BREATHI

BREATHING, I PRAY

Christian answer boldly,
'While I breathe, I pray:'
J. M. Neale[1]

IVAN MANN

DARTON·LONGMAN+TODD

First published in 2005 by
Darton, Longman and Todd Ltd
1 Spencer Court
140–142 Wandsworth High Street
London
sw18 4JJ

ISBN 0 232 52565 X

A catalogue record for this book is available from the British Library.

Designed by Sandie Boccacci
Phototypeset in 9.5/12.5pt Palatino by Intype Libra Ltd, London
Printed and bound in Great Britain by
The Cromwell Press, Trowbridge, Wiltshire

Contents

ACKNOWLEDGEMENTS

THERE ARE TOO MANY PEOPLE TO THANK. I would have to begin with the people of St Stephen's Church, Norwich, where I first realised my faith. In later life I have been grateful to a succession of gifted spiritual directors – Eilish Heath, Lister Tonge, David Spicer and Alice Keenleyside.

I am grateful to Darton, Longman and Todd and especially to Virginia Hearn for encouraging the writing of this book. Also for her skill and clarity in editing.

I am fortunate in having colleagues who share this life of prayer with me and among them I owe special thanks to Mags Blackie, whose own faith and prayer has helped me better understand my own.

Finally let me thank Carole Cormack. Her picture *Asteroid* immediately spoke to me of the joy and wonder of prayer and I am grateful for her permission to use it as the cover picture.

IVAN MANN
June 2004

PREFACE

THIS BOOK IS AN EMBARRASSMENT. The only way I have found it possible to write is to believe nobody will read it. At the same time I have had to write it as if I am writing it for you – the single and unique reader.

I began writing a fairly 'safe' book on prayer but as I prayed myself through the book I sensed that I was going to have to cover areas of prayer that may feel 'unsafe' to others. The earlier chapters, therefore, cover some of the better known ways of praying. The later chapters look at deeper themes of how prayer and life have inter-related in quite personal and difficult ways.

What this book tries to do is to be an honest account of the experience of prayer as it has been for me. My aim is not that you might imitate my prayer – it seems to me that one of me is enough. It has sometimes been a struggle I would not wish you to experience. No, my aim is that in seeing the connections between prayer and life for me you may be challenged and encouraged to see the connections between prayer and life in your own experience and so be inspired to live both more fully for the glory of God.

Chapter 1

REFLECTION AND MEANING

I WAS WALKING THE WELSH HILLS. It was towards the end of a long retreat and I felt as though God were trying to show me something but that I was too blind or too aloof to see. So I kept walking. My mind wandered back to my early life and to being a four-year-old who had severe speech difficulties – my 'L's sounded like 'Y's and my 'R's were 'W's, not to mention the other less definable sounds that made my speech opaque to the unpractised ear. For others it could be amusing – my father rejoiced in hearing me say that the dog was 'yicking' me or that I wanted an ice 'yoyyy'.

Reflecting on that time as I walked, I was reminded too of a visit to a speech therapist. She sat behind a desk and insisted I talk to her. The more she insisted the less I could say. We gave up after a couple of visits and the speech impediment and I were left to sort ourselves out. The effect was to make me a quiet child. I chose not to speak unless I had to – afraid of the need to keep repeating myself before anyone understood.

All through my life my speech has been a cause of concern, and though generally much better, when I am tired or low the old speech patterns re-emerge. Not surprisingly then, as I walked those Welsh hills and prayed I reflected on how I had seen my speech as an impediment to life and found myself asking God the meaning of it all. The answer that seemed to come caught me off guard and it took a while to believe it. The reality was that my inability to speak clearly added to my predisposition to be an introvert and combined to make me a very reflective person. If I could not express myself outwardly then I began to express myself inwardly – and to have a rich inner life whatever the outer circumstances.

As I spoke to God about this I realised that in going inward I had found him – that even as a four-year-old I knew the presence of God in my life and I recognise that he carried me through my childhood and has carried me since. What felt like (and was for years) a major restriction in my life was also a gift – I found God by turning inward.

Over the years I have come to realise that these times of reflection on the past often give events new meaning and allow me to make better choices for the future.

Reflection

In a wonderful line of poetry T. S. Eliot writes about having an experience but missing its meaning. It is so easily done, rushing onto the next thing, neither learning from the past nor enjoying the present.

A large part of my prayer is reflecting on the ordinary events of life in an attempt to see life with the eyes of God – to try to find God's meaning in the everyday. From my past it is clear that this reflective living comes more naturally to me than to others, but as a gift our capacity to be self-reflective is one which can be nurtured. It means that we can, to an extent, educate ourselves by learning from what has happened to us before and seeing how our reactions to events have shaped the rest of our lives.

What then do I mean by reflection? Reflection is not repetition. It is not rehearsing an event over and over again, confirming our original view of that event, deepening our original understanding – maybe our prejudices. It is not just remembering in the sense of drawing the picture of that part of our lives like a faithful photograph. Reflection is something else. Reflection is reviewing our lives with an open heart, mind and spirit so that we might gain fresh insights into how our life has unfolded. To reflect in this way requires a gentle approach and, for believers, requires too that we hold alongside a reflection on our life, a reflection on the life of Jesus or our understanding of God and his ways.

> I would like to live
> as a river flows
> carried by the surprise
> of its own unfolding.[1]

The key to such reflection is, I believe, generosity of heart towards ourselves and an attitude of gentleness.

Have you ever watched somebody sit down at a table in a restaurant? They take a while to get comfortable and then slowly pick up the napkin. As they talk to their companion they hold it in mid-air and then gently pull to release the folds – before carefully laying it on their lap and stroking it to smooth out the creases. The whole act is therapeutic, an act of healing, in the midst of a busy day. It's an image that comes to mind whenever we get to a certain point in Psalm 119:130:

> The unfolding of your words gives light;
> it imparts understanding to the simple.

As we approach the unfolding of a napkin, so may we approach the unfolding of our lives and of our understanding of God. We hold both gently in our hands, watching over them with love and coming attentively to listen to the Spirit's song as God tries to help us see what he would have us see.

When life has been traumatic for us it is too easy to listen only to the crashing sounds – the pains that have been inflicted on us and which we have inflicted on others, the misunderstandings and betrayals that make our relationships go awry. We can listen to these for eternity and allow them to continue to build up our resentments or sense of victimisation . . . OR . . . we can listen beneath those loud aggressive sounds to the deeper sound of God trying to be heard above the din. If we do that there will be a dying in us of things we need to release and in the dying a reception of new life. This dying will not deny those darker things but will transform their energy into that which is life-giving. Somehow this deeper listening can allow us both to release and to receive – not to release the past or its impact on us, but to release us from bondage to it, release us for what is to come.

Later we will think more on this, but to illustrate this way of listening beyond the surface let me tell you about an experience on another retreat. This time I was on my first retreat since the death of my wife, Jackie. She had been ill for five years and left me with four young children. I found myself in prayer asking God what I needed to see. Quite simply the answer came: 'There is joy in the heart of suffering.' I felt a strong physical revulsion. I feel it still as I remember the event. My head involuntarily started swinging 'No' from side to side. It felt, though, as if God held my head still and invited me to look. That afternoon I sat and wrote an account of those five years. At the end of twenty pages I wrote,

> . . . my story is not one of victory over suffering – but one of God's abiding presence – he who knew us before we were born and loves us with an everlasting love.
>
> Even in sorrow I have, in Him, found joy – a mystery to be lived.
>
> I take my hands away from before my face and hold them to God.

It was only looking back that I could see this so clearly – only by reflecting with God that I gained fresh meaning to those years of my life.

Meaning

We only have to scan several newspapers to realise that the same basic story can be conveyed with a wide range of interpretations. It's apparent too in the four gospels – how each has interpreted the story as they knew it to make their own theological point. Yet we so often settle for only a single view of our own life story – of our own gospel – our own good news of God in our lives. Consciously or subconsciously, we give meaning to our experience and sometimes stop too soon – 'been there, done that, got it taped' – but have we? Have we really learnt all we could have done from that betrayal, that rejection, that sudden burst of joy?

The meaning we give will often reflect our view of ourselves, of other people and of God. So one person may see illness as a sign of a punishing God. Another, believing in a God of infinite love, may question where God is or may see the presence of God in those who care. The meaning we give our experience is important. It can change our hopes for the future and our way of living.

Of all the books I have read, one that stands out for me is a book by Viktor Frankl called *Man's Search for Meaning*. In it he argues that we are not destroyed by suffering but by suffering without meaning. It can even be argued that the final choices we can make when life seems totally against us, are the choices about the meaning we give that experience. Meanings rather than meaning – for there may be layers of meaning in a single experience, and certainly different people may give perfectly valid different meanings to the same event. So much depends not only on the images we hold, but on the pattern of our life before and after an event. Often, then, we do not understand any pattern at all until we look backwards and gain the perspective of time.

In the gospels there are times when the disciples wait until they are alone with Jesus before they ask him what's going on. So with us, often it is when we spend time alone with Jesus that we can look back and review with him what life has held for us and how it fits into the dynamic of living and dying which is the Christ-life in us. It is then that new facets of meaning may pour light and hope into the darkest of lives. Sitting alongside the dying is often a privilege from this point of view. Those who know they are dying, and are given the gift of being able to be comfortable and relaxed, may work through the fears and anxieties to a time of acceptance and a time of seeing what life has been. It seems a pity to me that we do not make time for that earlier in life. In fact, often, times spent on retreat fulfil something of that role. We will return to the role of retreats in Chapter 16.

Choices

Whether we grow as a result of experience is often the result of choices we make. Brian Keenan and John McCarthy were often quick to remind each other that we always have choices – choices about how we react, choices about meaning assigned. We also have different ways of growing. Sometimes we grow by moving *beyond* current constraints; sometimes we grow by learning new ways of living *within* them. I have written before about the experience of watching someone whose life was severely limited by a stroke finding that music was a way of communication when other means of communication had failed.[2] It's a matter then of thinking broadly about possibilities and trusting others to help us when we cannot see the way ahead ourselves.

What has this to do with prayer? In the Old Testament there is a famous episode where Moses says to God's people that he lays before them a choice – life or death – and he advocates choosing life (Deuteronomy 30:19). The choice of life is the choice for God. It is the response of the prayerful. Fancy that! Maybe we have to dare to dance rather than look sombre, maybe we have to flirt a bit rather than become dry and cut off. Maybe we have to risk and trust rather than play safe. All this is prayer, prayer that desires life and desires God. Personally I am not very good at it. I have too often played safe and too seldom taken hold of life as though it were all gift, but I am slowly learning.

Much of the ability to take risks with prayer depends on believing that God is still labouring for us, and that he gives us life as a gift to be enjoyed. It depends on believing that God will not reject us if we are not always earnest but sometimes just rejoice in his gifts. It's the difference between a child who has been taught dutifully to say 'Thank you' for a present and the one who may be just as dutiful but who shows their gratitude in deeds by enjoying the gift they have been given.

It also demands an inner freedom that doesn't equate choosing God with a severe and over-demanding religiosity. If God wants us to give everything he doesn't want us to give our selves as desiccated people but as people flowing with the juices and energies of life – people who enjoy his creation and spread their enjoyment out of gratitude rather than guilt.

What helps me along this path is to remind myself that I am held in God's hand whatever I do. Julian of Norwich's *Revelations of Divine Love* often comes to my aid. In Chapter 5 she says (and I para-phrase): 'In his hand God holds us, in his love he enfolds us and he will never let us go.' In a more biblical mood I go back to that promise, 'I will not fail you or forsake you' (Deuteronomy 31:6). We do not have to be good to be loved by God. We simply have to live our lives directed towards him. Should we do good we shall help build the Kingdom. Should we sometimes fail but remember to turn back, he will be waiting for us as the father waited for the wayward son (Luke 15).

We have choices to make – but our salvation does not depend on making every choice the perfect one. Our salvation hangs only on learning to turn back to God whatever we have done – finding often that he has forgiven us already. We won't be wayward for its own sake if we love God because we do not by choice hurt those we love. But sometimes we make choices which do cause hurt and we have to believe that God forgives those too.

Choices are important but they are not, individually, the means of our salvation. God is the means and the choice he makes for us, his 'Yes' to us, means that he chooses us as his children. He gazes at us longingly with love and hopes we will respond to his choice of us by our choosing always to come back to him – by joining ourselves to the 'Yes' of his Son, whose 'Yes' shows us the way of living with a zest for real life.

Day to day

Reflection, meaning, choices – these are big themes which will be explored later in the book, but to be practical what do they mean for our prayer life and our living on a day-to-day basis? For me they mean the practice of reflecting on life so that we become more finely tuned to the ways of God.

As a boy I used to watch my father mend TVs and radios. I was fascinated by those dials where a marker moved along a line. First you would hear discordant hissing and then distorted sounds before the line was in the exact place where clarity would come. For years now I have been practising a way of praying which helps us 'tune in', to be sensitive to the movement of God's spirit in our lives. It's an exercise which is not foolproof (self-deception is always a risk) and which depends upon being open and honest with oneself. Quite simply it's a matter of placing yourself in the presence of an embracing and loving God and then letting the past twenty-four hours run through your mind. As you do so, ask God to show you where you feel there have been moments of life, love and energy. Nurture these moments; enjoy them again. Be like a child who tears open the paper, opens the present, plays with the toy enthusiastically, stops briefly to run up, hug you and say thanks, only to return to the toy. Be like that with God. Really nurture those moments of gift.

Another way to highlight these moments is to ask God to show you times in the day where you are aware of being loved or being given the ability to love. Again, enjoy those moments. Relish them, savour them and thank God for them.

Being human is also about making mistakes and sometimes hurting people or failing to live the life we feel called to live. We don't need to make a great fuss about those times. Just recognise them, say sorry and turn again to God. If our saying sorry reflects an inward disposition to seek to be loving we will naturally try not to repeat avoidable incidents again. This part of the exercise always reminds me of the Flanders and Swann song about the hippopotamus. So often we make of sin an excuse to wallow in mud. Rather, we need to just recognise it and steer clear next time.

Then finally, as we come to the end of this exercise, which may take only a few minutes, we ask God for strength for the next day – to live more fully his way.

This exercise helps us reflect and see the meaning of our days and moments. In that reflection we may make choices for the future. It's an ongoing task – a simple way of offering each day to God.[3]

Chapter 2

CHEWING THE CUD

THE PHRASE OF MUSIC KEPT GOING THROUGH MY MIND, 'Come away fellow sailors, come away . . .' It was beginning to irritate and I tried to distract myself to other thoughts. Eventually I took the hint and wondered whether my psyche or God (or both) were trying to tell me something. It was the beginning of a time of prayer that affirmed that I was a beloved child of God. I should have known. God has often used just a few words to attract my attention. On another day at about the same time I heard myself singing, 'If you go away . . .', a song I remember from years ago being sung by Judith Durham. In my prayer it related to a life without God and at first left me feeling desolate but then full of desire for a closer relationship.

Over the years I have grown accustomed to listening to these deeper resonances – not just ignoring the odd word, phrase or snippet of music but sometimes stopping to 'chew the cud', to let them speak more profoundly.

It's part of my natural reflective attitude to life but only came consciously to be part of my prayer in my late twenties. By then I had been ordained for a year or two. I went to see my bishop to ask who could help me develop a life of prayer. He mentioned the name of a sister in Oxford – Mother Mary Clare SLG. I had no idea who she was and it was with some trepidation that I arranged to see her.

She turned out to be a woman in her eighties, sitting in a wheelchair with a cat on her lap. She belonged to the Community at Fairacres in Oxford – the Sisters of the Love of God. As soon as I saw her I realised that she had once visited my theological college. She'd given a talk on prayer and afterwards I couldn't remember a word she had said but remembered her for one thing – she made God feel near. Later I read a quote from her erstwhile friend

Archbishop Michael Ramsey, who said, 'there are some people who make God feel near and it's the greatest gift that one human being can give to another.' I often wondered whether he had her in mind.

She let me talk for almost an hour about my desire for God and for a more ordered life of prayer. She listened, really listened. She gave me no instruction in prayer. She simply recognised what was already happening naturally – I was using *Lectio Divina*, she said. So she placed my way of praying within the tradition and she suggested some reading to help me understand. It was all the affirmation I needed. It was the only time I saw her but enough to fan the flames of my desire to grow in prayer. In the end *Lectio Divina* is simply chewing the cud of Scripture. It is more than a method of prayer, it is a way of life. It begins not in words but in the meeting of hearts – ours and God's.

Let the word of Christ dwell richly in you

A meeting of hearts is a powerful encounter. Sometimes it takes us by storm. At other times it happens gently. We need to be aware of what is happening in us at such a time. St Ignatius of Loyola suggests that we should discern our feelings to see as clearly as we can whether what we feel is coming from God or from that which is not God.

Quite simply, if we are seeking God and wanting to serve him then God's spirit presents itself as gentle, stirring 'up courage and strength, consolations, tears, inspirations and tranquillity'. That which is not God will be experienced as 'gnawing anxiety' or sadness and there will be seeming obstacles to our following God's way.

If we are spurning God the spirits reverse and that which is not God seems delightful and God's spirit will be experienced as a stinging conscience.

Clearly, this is the briefest of outlines of only part of Ignatius' teaching but it makes clear that if we are seeking God and want to know, love and follow Christ the good spirit will often be experienced as gentle and life-giving. Sometimes I have imagined it as a feather on the breath of God – some movement in life which is discernible but only when I apply myself and all my senses fully to become aware of it.

Because it is often gentle, the way we approach Scripture needs to be gentle too.

In Chapter 1 the image of a napkin was used of our awareness of the unfolding of our life and our understanding of God. It is a good image, too, for an approach to Scripture.

Imagine, then, opening a napkin in a busy restaurant. You are with someone you love . . . trying to listen, amidst the many voices, to that one voice. You take up the napkin, and almost imperceptibly unfold it as you listen . . . your attention all the while on their face. So we are to read Scripture. Our attention is to be on the face of God, listening with our soul to him. We are listening for the gentle voice, the voice of love.

Desire for God

Looking back I realised that I had been doing that for years – almost by instinct. As a boy I was tall for my age so when my eight-year-old brother joined the local church choir I joined too – a touch of 'Anything you can do, I can do better.' In the choir I caught a vision of what life with God could be like. Looking back, two streams of thought strike me still. Despite my inability to understand much of what we sang I had a sense of desire for God. Psalm 42 spoke profoundly to me:

> Like as the hart desireth the waterbrooks
> so longeth my soul after thee O God.
> My soul is athirst for God, yea, even for the living God.

or, in the hymn:

> As pants the hart for cooling streams
> when heated in the chase
> so longs my soul, O God for thee . . .

These phrases of the psalm have been quietly working away in my soul now for forty-five years and still they draw me.

The other glimpse I had was through the experience of walking towards the West end of the church at the end of a summer Evensong. As we walked towards the setting sun flooding through the window we sang:

As o'er each continent and island
The dawn leads on another day
The voice of prayer is never silent
Nor dies the strain of praise away.

This vision of continual prayer moved me deeply and, though I would go out of church to be one of the choirboys playing practical jokes with the rest, I would remember those glimpses.

Prayer was drawing me. Later in life I would see how prayer was an attraction from my earliest years and though I still do not find structuring prayer easy I am aware that I pray in the oddest of places – I just find myself talking to God or aware of his presence. In my life I had found a voice that could be heard, a face that attracted me. I had learnt to listen to the voice and watch the face. Praying with Scripture naturally became my way of prayer – and chewing the cud is a large part of it.

Reading a letter

Imagine sitting on a bus or the Tube and everyone who has a book or paper is reading aloud. That's how reading was in earlier times. The monks and nuns reading Scripture would pronounce it with their lips, hear it with their ears and see it with their eyes. They called it 'listening to the voices of the pages'. It is a good image of what reading Scripture can be about – listening to the voices of the pages – not just the words but listening too to the deeper resonances – God's meaning for us. I like to imagine that, as those who follow Jesus, we listen not only to the words but to the heartbeat of Christ in them. It is as though God breathed into the words (2 Timothy 3:16, All Scripture is God-breathed, NIV) and when we read them slowly and with generosity he breathes out of them – not necessarily through a sterile repetition of the words but by allowing them to speak to us today, primarily through the experience of an encounter with the divine.

One way of describing it is to imagine Scripture to be a love letter from God. When a phrase stands out in a letter we tend to ponder it during the day. We may wonder what was meant by a phrase. What did it convey? What did it not say? So we talk of reading between the lines – trying to be sensitive to deeper realities and not just the bare script in front of us. Reading Scripture in this way can be highly illuminating. It can allow God to speak afresh to us, to breathe new life into us, to allow us to encounter not just words but Word – Jesus himself.

Lectio Divina

What I hope is clear from the preceding is that *Lectio Divina* is not just a method of prayer. It is something we do naturally to a greater or lesser extent and which we can develop in our prayer life.

It is a very human activity – just like reading a letter – so before you read Scripture you contemplate the person who sent it, in this case, God. How is God looking at you and how are you looking at him? As you become aware, though not necessarily feeling, that you are in God's presence, imagine that gaze of love. Then lift your book – it may be Scripture or some other source of spiritual reading – and read the passage with which you are to pray. Read it as though it were a *love* letter from God. It doesn't need to be finished quickly. It just needs to be read as though you are expecting personal communication. Then when you have read the passage stop and see whether any word, phrase or image stands out.

Let that which has attracted you begin to take hold of you. If it's a word or phrase repeat those words aloud, then in your mind, until they slowly drop into your being, your heart – that place in you which God has made for encountering him. There the words begin to stir up thoughts and feelings. Listen to them, respond to them and when you are ready talk to God about them. These are the materials of prayer.

When you sense that it's time to move on either bring the prayer period to a close or, if you have more time, read the passage a little further and see whether there is more material for prayer. Finally, close the prayer period by words of thanksgiving or a short prayer.

It can sound very soothing and relaxing. Sometimes it is. Sometimes it's like watching a feather blown by a breeze. The words somehow touch us gently and we gain understanding. At other times words of comfort give way to deeper feelings. I am reminded of a lady who found herself praying with 'Do not be afraid'. For three days she was comforted but, underneath, something else was happening. On the fourth day she found herself arguing with God, raging at him, why should she not be afraid? Given her life history and experience her fear was not unreasonable. But talking to God she found compassion and fresh understanding, allowing her to move on.

Personal letters

Reading Scripture in this way makes Scripture personal. There will be phrases that stay with us for a lifetime and take us back to experiences of God's closeness and to the memory of what God meant for us at key points in our life. It connects Scripture, prayer and life.

Let me take you back to the time when my wife was ill with Motor Neurone Disease. Three key passages of Scripture became incredibly meaningful and still reduce me to awe – words from Philippians, Jeremiah and Matthew's gospel.

Philippians

The letter to the Philippians has often spoken to me. I love the passage in chapter 3 where it says,

> Yet whatever gains I had, these I have come to regard as loss because of Christ. More than that, I regard everything as loss because of the surpassing value of knowing Christ Jesus my Lord. For his sake I have suffered the loss of all things, and I regard them as rubbish, in order that I may gain Christ and be found in him, not having a righteousness of my own that comes from the law, but one that comes through faith in Christ, the righteousness from God based on faith. I want to know Christ and the power of his resurrection and the sharing of his sufferings by becoming like him in his death, if somehow I may attain the resurrection from the dead. (Philippians 3:7-11)

When Jackie was ill this passage would often come to mind. Her illness, being progressive and degenerative, made us face the reality of her death. Whilst others would try to deny that reality and wanted to convince us that trust in God would be enough to heal her, we had a different view. We had both prayed over a long period before we dared to voice it to each other. We both realised that our invitation was to accept the truth of this illness and live and grow through it. So another verse from Philippians came to be my ally:

'For he has graciously granted you the privilege not only of believing in Christ, but of suffering for him as well' (Philippians 1:29). It was not that we thought God sent us suffering – but we did believe that in accepting the suffering which came our way and offering it and ourselves for God it could be used and we could be transformed by sharing the power of the resurrection in offering our suffering to God. When Jackie died another verse from Philippians came to mind for the headstone – 'In life and death Christ glorified.'

Lectio Divina then is not a prayer exercise somehow separate from life. It is a prayer lived. It can be a means of maintaining hope in the darkest moments.

Jeremiah

Jackie and I were not saints. It is easier to write about how we felt called to accept suffering than it was to live it. Often I would scream at God, scream at the injustice of it all. I would quake with anger when she died and people kindly said, 'It's a blessing after all those years.' I would writhe with knowing that four children did not have a mother. Our acceptance was real but not without cost. Looking back, another passage punctuated my life at that time. It is a passage from Jeremiah:

> For surely I know the plans I have for you, says the LORD, plans for your welfare and not for harm, to give you a future with hope. Then when you call upon me and come and pray to me, I will hear you. When you search for me, you will find me; if you seek me with all your heart, I will let you find me, says the LORD. (Jeremiah 29:11-14)

I cannot describe the importance of these words. I remember going out one evening when I was at a low ebb. A friend had offered to babysit and I went to a group run by some friends. It was an informal group of Christians who met for mutual companionship and sometimes prayed together, read Scripture together or simply relaxed together. That evening the host said he had decided to invite us to ponder a few words of Scripture. These were the words – words which had already spoken to me many times, but of that our host knew nothing.

He began to read. I flooded with tears. Here at the depth of my pain came words which spoke profoundly.

Later in life, reading again about Jeremiah's life and the conflict in his call, I found the words again resonating as I prayed through conflict in my own call. Somehow these words have become a symbol of God's transforming power, drawing me through struggle to life. They are a reminder that God is present and active even in the midst of all that happens.

Matthew

For months at a time during that period I found myself so exhausted by giving twenty-four hour care that I could hardly pray. In my journal I record spasmodically what was going on. One word stands out – Emmanuel. 'God-with-us.' It seemed to be enough some days just to hold that word. It didn't stop the anger, frustration or exhaustion but it gave a different texture to the day and made it somehow sustainable.

It constantly surprised me that even though life was more than full, demanding in every way, this one word would keep returning to the surface of my mind and heart and act as a support. I did not even consciously intend to use it for prayer. It had begun to pray itself – much as the Jesus Prayer does. (More about that in Chapter 6.)

Fragility

More and more I have discovered that this is how it works – God's approach is gentle. There may be a word or a few words. If we are attentive then those words will be transformative in our lives. No wonder that listening, awareness, is at the heart of the spiritual life. That great Jewish prayer that Jesus heard at Mary's knee says it all – *Hear*, O Israel . . .

Listen – and to be able to hear the voice of God is itself a grace, a grace we can pray to receive. I love that passage in Isaiah: 'Morning by morning he wakens – wakens my ear to listen as those who are taught' (Isaiah 50:4b).

We are invited to listen and to listen not only with our ears but with the ears of our heart to all that is outside us and to all that is within – using all that we are – hearing, sight, feel, touch and smell . . . opening our very selves to be receptive to God.

What will we hear?

Maybe it will be a few words from Scripture or from some other spiritual reading. Maybe it will be a few words of a song or of a film or TV show. What we hear from God is often fragile. We could easily miss it but if we realise some words have spoken to us we can reflect on them and through them listen to the fragile voice at the heart of creation that says, 'I love you, come to me.'

In my own life I have so often listened to the other voices – 'voices which so easily convince us of our inner darkness and lead us to lose touch with God whose nature we share'.[1] I had failed to hear the gentler voice of God – the voice that says, 'I love you (without conditions) . . . come to me.' I have to keep reminding myself to listen to God's voice, to look at his face, 'for his voice is sweet and his face is lovely' (cf. Song of Solomon 2:14).

Again, in Ignatius' writing I found an image that helped. He speaks of God's spirit being like a good angel touching the soul gently and lightly like water dropping onto a sponge, and the spirit which is not God being sharp, disturbing and noisy like water falling onto a stone – or, as a friend of mine puts it, like rain on a tin roof.

Maybe God will come to you in thunder, lightning, smoke and fire – a divine Hollywood – or maybe he will come more gently – in a fragile way. You may hear him or not hear him . . . Listen with all you are. Practise listening with all your senses – not by a concentrated urgent listening that deadens the other senses but in that relaxed listening which leaves all the senses receptive. Then, blessed are you. Happy your ears will be because they hear.

Chapter 3

PSALMS AND POETRY

IT'S STRANGE HOW, AS YOU GO THOUGH LIFE, your interests change. As a lad I used to enjoy the practical things – being up on the roof helping my father secure TV aerials, or messing around with car engines. At school too I was seen as someone who loved mathematics and physics – subjects that were practical and down to earth. It wasn't until I was fifteen and had already failed an English GCE that the English teacher told me the best preparation for the re-sit would be to start to read more. I began to read and much to my surprise discovered that I not only liked it but loved it. I couldn't read enough. I was yet to enter the world of poetry, though. That came later, but looking back I realise that some of my love of language found its foundation in worship – in some of the hymns and in the psalms.

When I got to theological college I remember the shock of going to a seminar on the psalms as prayer. Few people seemed to get anything from them – whereas they had been feeding me for years – though often I had not recognised at the time that they were. Reviewing my life now I realise how at times a psalm has been crucial in my development – drawing me back to God.

One such psalm is a common favourite – Psalm 139. As I have come to recognise the hand of God in my upbringing and life so this psalm speaks of that love extending to before my birth – and of course extending to you before your birth.

> You created my inmost self,
> knit me together in my mother's womb . . .
> You knew me through and through . . .
> when I was being formed in secret,
> textured in the depths of the earth.[1]

Often, when I have needed to ground myself once more in God I have returned to this psalm. At other times I have been captivated by a verse from Psalm 27:

> 'Come,' my heart says,
> 'seek his face!'
> Your face, LORD, do I seek.

Here is rich material for *Lectio Divina*, a source of deep prayer. Once, when on a retreat where we took no props at all[2] – no Bible, books, radio, or literature of any kind – I wondered what I would find to pray with. What surfaced in my mind more often than not were words from a psalm and the days passed easily as they resonated within me and led to prayer.

I am grateful for those early days in the choir and for the repetition of the words so that they became part of me, but even for people without those childhood memories, I believe the psalms read slowly and meditatively are a way into acknowledging the full range of human emotions before God.

Alongside the psalms I have found poetry to be another good way of chewing the cud. A recent experience is not uncommon for me. I was in a bookshop waiting for others to make their choices and so found myself casually browsing. I picked up a book of poetry, opened it randomly, and came across a few words that stayed with me for several weeks:

> I phoned from time to time to see if she's
> changed the music on her answerphone.
> 'Tell me in two words,' goes the recording,
> 'what you were going to tell in a thousand.'[3]

Here were words, *Tell me in two words, what you were going to tell in a thousand*, which struck me profoundly and took me to an encounter with Christ. God having spoken his word through his prophets, mostly men, verbose wordy men, chose a woman, Mary, to bear his most beautiful, his most lovely Word. I was reminded too of St John of the Cross who famously said, 'One word spoke the Father and that Word is his Son and the word ever speaks in silence.' Even as I stood in the shop I found myself imagining what this meant – God speaks through his Son. His Word has a face and hands, a body, legs and eyes with which to see the Father's creation and lungs to breathe the Father's air. He has ears to hear the Father's music and a mouth to taste the Father's food and a nose to smell the sweet perfume of flowers and the heavy sweat of labour. God's Word takes human form.

'Look in the cradle,' Mary says and the neighbours peer over her shoulder and see this child. 'My, he looks like you,' says one . . . and another 'No, he's the spitting image of his dad,' and Mary smiles . . . just like his dad, like the eternal Father whose child she bore. One word spoke the Father, and that Word is his Son.

Such is the power of poetry in my prayer. It never ceases to amaze me. It is something again I cannot control – mostly it's a matter of coming across a poem and being struck by just a few words. The poem may be intentionally religious or completely secular in intention.

God touched me

As I reflect on which particular poems have been long-term friends, I realise it is often those that take me to the place of encounter with God – poems which draw me to look at Christ in a new way, or those which remind me that I have sometimes caught a glimpse of him. I went, for instance, on a counselling course where the speaker read a poem by R. S. Thomas:

> A memory of Kreisler once:
> At some recital in this same city,
> The seats all taken, I found myself pushed
> On to the stage with a few others,
> So near that I could see the toil
> Of his face muscles, a pulse like a moth
> Fluttering under the fine skin
> And the indelible veins on his smooth brow.
>
> I could see, too, the twitching of the fingers,
> Caught temporarily in art's neurosis,
> As we sat there or warmly applauded
> This player who so beautifully suffered
> For each of us upon his instrument.

So it must have been on Calvary
In the fiercer light of the thorns' halo:
The men standing by and that one figure,
The hands bleeding, the mind bruised but calm,
Making such music as lives still.
And no one daring to interrupt
Because it was himself that he played
And closer than all of them the God listened.[4]

The speaker's point was about listening but she had made it almost impossible for me to listen to her any more – I was stuck with an image of Christ on the cross – 'it was himself that he played'. The poem had drawn me to look at Christ afresh.

A day on the beach at Southwold takes me to the other kind of poetry – the kind that reminds me that I have glimpsed God. On the way to the beach I stopped in a second-hand book shop and bought a copy of poetry by Gerard Manley Hopkins. I only read a few lines and I was captivated by God – 'over again I feel thy finger and find thee'.[5] R. S. Thomas draws me too when he writes, 'I looked at him not with the eye only but with the whole of my being, overflowing with him, as a chalice would with the sea.'[6]

In a way, when God comes to me through poetry I often sense an incalculable gift. Like all grace it is not something I can engineer – I can read poetry books all evening and nothing strikes me. Alternatively, as we have seen, I can glance through a book and be lifted to an intimacy I long for.

The psalms and poetry, then, can be a means of evoking prayer. They can, for me, also be a way of praying.

Writing poetry

Writing poetry has often been, for me, a way of breaking the silence when I cannot pray. Having gone through a dark period of life I attended a workshop on St John of the Cross. The theory about John's life and writings did not touch me greatly but his poetry did. As I sat to pray I found myself writing:

    Isolation,
    Pain,
    Emptiness

Crucible of Life
Crucified
Pinned down by circumstance
Immobile
Still.

Interior Scream
Sounding,
Bouncing,
Colliding with the crucified
Until
From the stones,
Sapphires are found
And from the dust,
Spangles of gold.

Rich treasury
Resourcefulness
Sheer grace of boundless love
Found only in the night.

O generous dark
O God
I love you.

If some of my poetry stems from places of pain, it also leaps out of
the presence of sheer grace. There was an evening, for example,
where a regular church group suddenly opened up to a deeper
honesty and human support for one another. I found myself,
afterwards, overwhelmed by a recognition of the presence of God:

There are no words,
they hang, like ill-fitting coats,
upon an awe
which only speaks
in SILENCE.
There are no words.
Only a Word,
a presence,
which blows in by His

choosing
and scatters graces
eagerly upon us.
There are no words.
Instead, the music of eternity
played out in
silent love,
and we are lost in Him.

Such poems are not great works of art but they do create a flow
where insights can emerge and then be prayed over. They can take
a daily habit – taking the dog on the beach, for instance – and make
it a moment of eternity:

The 'chauffeur' edges
round the car,
opening the door,
respectfully.
One must demur.

The dog is going for a walk.

The short conveyance to the road
that runs beside the beach and then
excitement!
Man and dog
tails wagging
head for the sun
listening to the larks
tasting the air
embracing the breeze
hearts racing with God's life.

A new day is born.

Writing psalms

In the build-up to the war in Iraq I found myself wondering what a
psalm for today would say. Psalms, of course, cover a wide range of
emotions and situations but I long in our liturgy and prayer to hear

psalms written for today. I so often find myself wanting to articulate a response to the horrors of the news without just hearing another prayer for the situation . . . I want to learn again how to lament.

In a remarkable little book Nicholas Wolterstorff reflects on the death of his son in a mountain climbing accident. A friend told him that he had given copies of this book, *Lament for a Son*, to each of his children. Wolterstoff asked him why he had done that. 'Because it is a love song.'[7] Every lament is a love song. It is a yearning for something better, something beyond what is currently experienced. Though it may begin as a longing for what has been, it often longs too for what shall be. A lament is not content with what is. It is an act of rebellion, an act of revolt. But, furthermore, lament can be the means by which we move on – a means by which the centre moves from our own concerns to God, first in anger and recrimination but maybe later in wide-eyed wonder. Wolterstorff writes:

> How is faith to endure, O God, when you allow all this scraping and tearing on us? You have allowed rivers of blood to flow, mountains of suffering to pile up, sobs to become humanity's song – all without lifting a finger that we could see. You have allowed bonds of love without number to be painfully snapped. If you have not abandoned us, explain yourself.
>
> We strain to hear. But instead of hearing an answer we catch sight of God himself scraped and torn. Through our tears we see the tears of God . . . [8]

Lament is the place of encounter with the deepest mysteries and with the present God. No wonder Jesus turns to Psalm 22 – 'My God, My God, why have you abandoned me.' As Harry Williams says, he meant it too. He was not just saying the afternoon office. He felt the abandonment and he utters it in full frontal honesty.

In the five years of looking after Jackie I wrote only one piece of poetry and it was lament, articulating the enormous and brutal pain of being a carer, whilst affirming a sense of God's presence.

I like full frontal honesty before God, not just in lament but in praise. One of the exercises that helped me come to terms with nursing someone who was terminally ill was, as I reflected later, to ponder Psalm 136, which gave rise to the following:

O give thanks to the Lord for he is good
For his steadfast love endures forever.
O give thanks to God for those who care
For his steadfast love endures forever.
O give thanks to the Lord for times of humour and fun
For his steadfast love endures forever.
O give thanks for the children's resilience
For his steadfast love endures forever.
O give thanks for a glimpse of truth
For his steadfast love endures forever.
O give thanks that he has been there for us before
For his steadfast love endures forever.
O give thanks that he will be again
For his steadfast love endures forever.
O give thanks to the God of truth
For his steadfast love endures forever.
O give thanks for love before the foundation of the
    world
For his steadfast love endures forever.
O give thanks for love reaching into eternity
For his steadfast love endures forever.

These laments and psalms of praise are not escapes from reality –
they are glimpses into different sides of the same reality, glimpses
into the presence of God. I encourage others to write them too. They
are part of our salvation history – part of the journey of faith, and if
we read them at future dates they take us back immediately to these
moments. I have a file of forty or fifty of them spanning twenty
years.

Indeed in writing this chapter I have re-read them and been
moved to tears of love as I discover in them a desire for God beyond
my ability to conceive or create.

They remind me that *in offering truth* to God I grow. They are
channels by which God speaks specifically to the circumstances of
my life and they allow me to respond:

> Lord, you are the sculptor and I the work of your
>   hands.
> I have assented to your skills,
> I have enjoyed the caress of your hands

and the life-blows of your making me.
You have used the whole of life to mould me to your
     praise . . .
but more . . . in the furnace of my passions and my
     pain,
you have carved out a place within me for yourself,
you have enlarged my heart,
and the carving out has cost me
not less than everything
and yet
I have assented
wanting only your love . . .

Father,
from stone you have fashioned flesh,
and, in a twinkle given it breath
I had no choice.
It was your 'yes'.
But now I consent
bear me again, give birth to me
that I may birth your Son for those I serve.
Shape me by the blows and joys of life.
Chisel me intricately as once you knit me,
nurtured me in the womb.
Smooth me gently with your love as once you
     quietened my baby soul.
Shape me, conform me, to your Son
carve out in me a great space for yourself,
my living heart
that those who come to me may find
your love
your compassion.

Textured in the womb
I was held in love's embrace.
Birth, not seeking my assent,
abandoned me to life.
Death, too, will come not at my choosing
but at yours, my God,
and dying I will again be abandoned but then to LIFE.

So it is now,
the present moment,
only
that I choose,
give my consent
to be abandoned, feckless, love filled.
It is now I choose to give assent to life,
to you, my God.

Chapter 4

IMAGINATION

Despite my growing love of poetry and of conjuring up potent images, there remains in me a strong sense that I find work easier than play. Imagination does not come easily. I am too rooted in the reality of the present moment to let go to flights of fantasy. Yet there have been times in my life when imagination and prayer have been the agents of transformation.

It was coming into contact with Ignatian spirituality that brought the whole idea to the fore. I went on a retreat where I was invited to pray with Scripture – not in my preferred way of *Lectio Divina* but by actually imagining myself in a gospel scene. I was invited, for instance, to imagine taking Jesus down from the cross. As I tried to pray I did not believe that much would happen. In terms of visual images I have little imagination, but I was stunned to discover that if I used all my senses I could feel what it would be like to take Jesus from the cross; I could imagine what it would mean to me to hold his body, even though I could not imagine the scene visually. I also discovered that I could imaginatively enter into conversation with other people there.

As a result of that retreat and my discovery of this different way of praying, which helped me, I went on to other retreats, to praying the Ignatian *Spiritual Exercises* in daily life and then to a full thirty-day Ignatian retreat. Cumulatively these things changed my life so now, in the light of these experiences, I no longer discard imagination as a means of prayer!

Later in the chapter we will look specifically at how we pray with Scripture, but I have also found that God uses my imagination to see ordinary objects as the means of prayer. What I have discovered is that these flights of fancy can be of more help than long and arid explanations of how to pray. People still talk to me, fifteen years on, of folding in egg whites, of covering a situation with custard or of following a feather. Images speak.

Egg whites

At a time when I had responsibility for cooking for the family – and was fairly new to the game – I came to a grinding halt when a recipe said, 'Fold in the egg whites'. I couldn't quite understand what they could mean. Origami with egg whites was beyond me.

Only later did I make the connection with prayer. So often in life, in worship and in prayer, we are struck by something either discordant or joyful. It may be a memory or a sense of being translated to another experience of life – a certain smell may take us back to school dinners, or to a time in hospital. These slight but powerful memories and insights can so easily be dismissed.

Why did watching that film reduce us to tears? And why did walking into that room with that particular smell take us back to being a three-year-old?

When people go on retreat and enter silence for several days they often become very sensitive to those times of awareness. It's then that I often find myself talking about egg whites. Rather than rush into praying with something else, I suggest they take those feelings and that awareness, and fold it all, very gently, back into the prayer.

Often, these are the ways in which God is trying to make himself known to us, in his gentle, unassuming, courteous way. If we get carried away by the force of the feelings evoked in us, we may miss the gentle voice of love. The Vulgate version of the 'still small voice' is 'the whistling of a gentle air'. As people tell me about the 'storm' of emotions or the 'clamour' of the past, I try to stay still within, so that, through it all, I may hear this whistling gentle air – it is this voice which often tells us most clearly how God is looking at us with love through it all.

Feather

In recent years Hildegard of Bingen has become better known. A woman who lived through four-fifths of the twelfth century, Hildegard was probably one of the most influential woman of her day. She was a woman of tremendous stature and power who used her gifts to the utmost, and her gifts were many.

In 1106 Hildegard, aged eight, was given by her parents, 'into the hands of Jutta', the abbess of a community of women attached to the Benedictine monastery of Disibodenberg, near Bingen, about twenty-five miles south-west of Mainz. When Jutta died, Hildegard succeeded her as abbess. She saw tongues of flames descend from the heavens and settle upon her.

Not given to accepting less than she thought God required, she took her sisters, along with their dowries, away from the monastery and in 1151 they moved into a new cloister built for them in Rupertsberg, near the town we know as Bingen. She faced, as a result of this move and also because of some of her writing and preaching, a great deal of opposition, but she was resilient. Paradoxically, she sees herself not as a tough old bird but as a gentle feather:

> Listen, there was once a king sitting on his throne. Around him stood great and wonderfully beautiful columns orna-mented with ivory, bearing the banners of the king with great honour. Then it pleased the king to raise a small feather from the ground and he commanded it to fly, not because of anything in itself but because the air bore it along. Thus am I . . .

This image has been, for me, a very powerful one – to be that avail-able for God, detached from protecting oneself unnecessarily, but simply attentive to God, present for him. Alan Neame describes it perfectly. He says, 'You think that loving God means giving him something? Give him access, that is all he requires, that is all he asks for: for loving God only means offering ourselves to the liberality of his love: it means letting him love us.'[1]

Give God access. Be his flexible friend, a feather on his breath:

> The words I speak come from no human mouth; I saw and heard them in visions sent to me . . . God moves where he wills, and not to the glory of earthly man. I am ever filled with fear and trembling. I have no confidence in my own capacities – I reach out my hand to God that he may carry me along as a feather is borne weightlessly by the wind.

Oranges

Over my life I must have read thousands of books. Among them there is one passage from one book that stands out, a paragraph that drew me into an awareness of God, that explained to me something that I had not understood about myself, and which I hear echoing in my mind often, though I read it several years ago. It's a passage written by Brian Keenan about his time as a hostage:

Another day. The Shuffling Acolyte and I take part in our daily ritual, that long short walk to the toilet. That same walk back and I am home again. I don't look any more at the food, knowing its monotony will not change, not even its place on my filthy floor . . . With calm, disinterested deliberation I pull from my head the filthy towel that blinds me, and slowly turn to go like a dog well-trained to its corner, to sit again, and wait and wait, forever waiting. I look at this food which I know to be the same as it always has been.

But wait. My eyes are almost burned by what I see. There's a bowl in front of me that wasn't there before. A brown button bowl and in it some apricots, some small oranges, some nuts, cherries, a banana. The fruits, the colours, mesmerize me in a quiet rapture that spins through my head. I am entranced by colour. I lift an orange into the flat filthy palm of my hand and feel and smell and lick it. The colour orange, the colour, the colour, my God the colour orange. Before me is a feast of colour. I feel myself begin to dance, slowly, I am intoxicated by colour. I feel the colour in a quiet somnambulant rage. Such wonder, such absolute wonder in such an insignificant fruit.

I cannot, I will not eat this fruit. I sit in quiet joy, so complete, beyond the meaning of joy. My soul finds its own completeness in that bowl of colour. The forms of each fruit. The shape and curl and bend all so rich, so perfect. I want to bow before it, loving that blazing, roaring orange colour . . . Everything meeting in a moment of colour and of form, my rapture no longer an abstract euphoria. It is there in that tiny bowl, the world recreated in that broken

bowl. I feel the smell of each fruit leaping into me and lift-
ing me and carrying me away. *I am drunk with something
that I understand but cannot explain. I am filled with a sense of
love. I am filled and satiated by it. What I have waited and
longed for has without my knowing come to me, and taken all of
me.*[2] (my italics)

This is how God is for me . . . someone who without my knowing it
comes and fills my desire. As Maria Boulding says, he is on the
inside of my longing and his desire is so much greater than mine:

> You yourself are the place of desire and need. All your
> love, your stretching out, your hope, your thirst, God is
> creating in you so that he may fill you. It's not your desire
> that makes it happen but his. He longs through your
> heart.[3]

That's it. Whatever I think I desire, in the end God's desire is
greater. When I thought I was being called to priesthood I thought
somehow it depended on me. Twenty years later I wrote,
'Priesthood is not something we hold as a possession. Rather,
priesthood is just the way that God holds us.' Similarly, my desire
for truth has made me realise that our search for truth becomes
much more an awareness that, in a deeper sense, the truth is seeking us out. *What I have waited and longed for has without my knowing
come to me, and taken all of me.*

Often when I see oranges all this is conjured up again.
Sometimes, though, just remembering the vividness of Keenan's
writing makes me enjoy the look, smell and colour of oranges for
their own sake.

In 1975 I read a book about Mother Teresa. Only one sentence
lodged itself in my memory (though the whole book inspired me):

> If you have
>   two loaves of bread
> Give one to the poor,
>   sell the other –
> And buy hyacinths
>   to feed your soul.[4]

I have discovered, through Keenan's speaking to my imagination, that oranges feed my soul.

Rubber bands

I think I have found the ultimate 'executive toy' for those who seek to follow Jesus and who want to understand their vocation to follow him, and maybe to pursue a vocation within that vocation – to follow him in a particular way.

It all began when I was thinking about the call of Matthew (Matthew 9:9-13). Matthew's vocation, at least by the account given, is clear. He hears the call and has the interior freedom to answer immediately. As saints go, he has get-up-and-go, *'and he got up and followed Jesus'*. But I guess his following wasn't always as easy as that, even at the practical level, and there would be times when his response was less full hearted, less energetic, when even a saint found it hard to get out of bed to pray, when the rubber band had less pulling power and the sheets were like glue.

What then of vocation? How has it been for us?

Maybe sometime in the past we became aware of God . . . something moved inside us . . . there was the inkling of a relationship. We felt ourselves somehow drawn towards him. Then we may have had no idea of the shape of our calling – just that he had, somehow, a part in our life. It is as though God let us feel the drawing of the bands of love that attracted us to him (cf. Hosea 11).

At another time we felt the rubber band more intensely, when God seemed to be nudging us to tell us that he was calling us to a particular way of expressing that relationship. We may have tried to keep away from feeling it, busying ourselves with other things, hoping the persistent nudge would be for someone else. We might have fought against it, stretching the rubber band as far as we could, spending all the Father had given us elsewhere. We might have chosen to step outside it all, to say 'No', to go our own way, but we didn't. But once we had said 'Yes' to this particular way of responding to the touch of love nothing could have prepared us for the experience of living out our vocation.

Nothing could have prepared us for how difficult it is to let go of self – the struggle that St Augustine catches so well: 'I was swept up to thee by thy beauty and torn away from thee by my own weight', nor for the discernment needed between letting go of self for Christ and letting go in a destructive way. In comparison, letting go of possessions costs little. Only the drawing of his love can release us.

At other times the rubber band seems slack and it is hard to move on.

Nothing could have prepared us for those times when our vocation wrapped itself around us like the hand of God, when it protected us and nurtured us through the storms and tribulations of our being stripped and opened to greater love – those times when our vocation was indistinguishable from the love which 'clothes us, enfolds us and embraces us, that tender love' which 'completely surrounds us never to let us go'.[5]

Nor could we have expected the times when the love 'that never lets us go' felt somehow like a restraint and we fought with all our will to get away, discovering only when we stopped fighting that it was love that held us.

Nothing could have prepared us for those times when we wanted to take the rubber band into our own hands and use it, like a child at the back of the class, to fire our own ego in its trajectory, to shout 'I AM', to make everyone notice our presence. But then we realised the words were not ours to grasp to claim equality with him. Surrendering again, we found 'I AM' within: Christ and our true selves, not grasped but given. It is his way.

Nothing could have prepared us for that sense that, not only were we bound to him but also to each other. Nor could we have expected that sense that the bands that joined us to each other would so often cross and hurt, for the sense that another's vocation, another's rubber band might make mine difficult to feel or follow.

Nothing could have prepared us for the recognition that we'd seen it with our eyes, not God's – that there were not separate bands, but one – the band of love woven by Christ in his incarnation, life and death, and resurrection. His band of love embraced the world and yet could focus on each one, his touch of love on me defining my vocation, his touch of love on you defining yours. All he asks is that we live truly that vocation which is uniquely ours.

And then our eyes were opened to the Father's band of love, the bands of love by which he led his people, the love by which he lifted them to his cheek, by which he bent down and fed them, by which he longed to seek the lost, to bind up the injured and strengthen the weak. And then we realised, within that love, that deep compassion, we do not come alone into the Kingdom, we come like Matthew, not with the righteous, but with fellow sinners.

But more, we realised that to live our vocation, to get up and go, however feebly, is somehow important for the world itself. Somehow, mysteriously, we play a part in answering the world's calling to be drawn by love, propelled by love, to follow Christ into eternity.

It's amazing what a rubber band can stimulate in prayer – another example of God being in all creation when our eyes are open and our imagination allowed to come into play.

And custard? It's what you put on rhubarb – a perfect image of how the whole of life should be covered in prayer.

Imagination and Scripture

All these images seem a long way from using imagination when praying with Scripture and yet they suggest a way of praying whereby we let something touch us and we go with the flow of it as we commit a time to God. Praying with the imagination involves both – it is more than going with the flow. It is going with the flow *with God*.

So when we pray with a passage – probably a gospel passage, we begin by realising that we are in God's loving presence and then commit the time of prayer to God – that it may be to God's praise and glory. The Ignatian tradition also suggests that we ask for some inward insight and gift – a grace – maybe simply to know Jesus more intimately and follow him more closely.

We then take our passage of Scripture, gently and lovingly – as that which comes from God's hand. Using all our senses we then enter the scene. If we were praying with the feeding of the five thousand we might imagine the setting – what kind of countryside, the colour of the sky and the shape of the hills. We might imagine the noise of a crowd and then picture Jesus and the small boy. We may talk to a character in the scene – Jesus, the boy or one of the disciples. For some people this imagining will be graphic and pic-torial. For me it is just a sense. Either way it is a means of entering the scene and then letting it speak to us.

For a while we let the scene unfold before us and let the con-versation flow. As our prayer time comes to an end we talk to

God about what has happened – as one would with a friend – and then bring our prayer time to a close.

It's all very simple but at its heart, as in all prayer, we seek an encounter with the living God – an encounter which will be transforming and full of life and love. It's worth using our imagination.

Chapter 5

JESUS PRAYER

WHEN I WAS IN TRAINING AS A THEOLOGICAL STUDENT I lived in Salisbury. As students we had a mixed reaction to the Church. We were about to be ordained and so to be inextricably linked with the Church for the rest of our lives. To keep balance and perspective we had nevertheless a questioning approach to the institution – and the questioning would sometimes just be a matter of poking fun.

Our bishop at the time was George Reindorp, a man who sometimes took being a bishop to the extremes. He not only wore the bishop's purple shirt (and socks), he also rode a purple push bike around the close. It was easy to make fun of him and yet I owe to him one of the most significant aspects of my prayer.

I went one Sunday to the cathedral and listened as he revealed to the congregation his own practice of using the Jesus Prayer. I heard that sermon in 1977 and now, over a quarter of a century later, I am still living with its impact. I am still using the Jesus Prayer as part of my spiritual life – or should I say it is using me as part of the spiritual life? As one Orthodox sister was fond of saying, 'The Jesus Prayer unfolds itself in the soul . . . after its own laws.'

Lord Jesus Christ, Son of God, have mercy on me

The Jesus Prayer is brief – even if the fuller version is used and one prays 'Lord Jesus Christ, Son of God, have mercy on me, *a sinner.*' It stems from the Orthodox tradition but has become widely used across denominations – especially since the publication in the nineteenth century of *The Way of a Pilgrim* by R. M. Trench. In essence, once we have used the prayer on a regular basis over a period of time it is a prayer which makes its home in us as Jesus too makes his home deep within us.

Apart from repeating the prayer the tradition suggests that one links it with breathing or with the heartbeat. It is a prayer that makes connections with the dynamic forces of life within us. It is, then, both a prayer for beginners and one which opens up our very heart to the work of grace and carries us to that which we most desire – union with God. At the end of this chapter we'll look at ways of beginning to use this prayer but, first, let me reflect on how it has become so important in my life.

After I heard that sermon, I began fairly self-consciously setting aside time to pray the Jesus Prayer – slowly and meditatively. I thought I would soon become holy! In fact it was boring and not much happened. Often I could not concentrate, the words appeared meaningless and it would have been easy to give up. Instead I looked back to the obvious depth of conviction with which George Reindorp had spoken – or was it God speaking to me through his words? Certainly I had a sense that this was important and worth pursuing. I began to say the prayer at odd moments too – when waiting at the bank or going for a walk.

I suppose it was about two years later that I stopped praying the prayer and it started praying in me. What do I mean? Quite simply that I found that from time to time I became aware of the words going through my soul. If I listened, they were praying away in me without my taking the initiative. That sense has lasted ever since. Often, as I calm down to go to sleep, I realise the prayer is going on. There is a sense in which it just happens and needs no encouragement from me. It is routine, uneventful and beautiful.

At other times in my life when prayer has seemed all but impossible it has been the saving grace. I turn to it as to an old friend and take refuge in it. At other times of great stress I have rested on its simplicity. Paradoxically, but not unexpectedly, it also rises to the surface at times of joy and peace.

I may be lying in the bath, walking beside a river in rural England or walking the streets of one of our major cities and still it is there – Lord Jesus Christ, Son of God, have mercy on me.

What is it then about this prayer that makes it so special? I believe it's to do with continual prayer, desire, the Jesus Prayer, the heart, and the person of Jesus.

Continual prayer

When we read that we should pray continually (1 Thessalonians 5:17) it seems like an impossible injunction. It's hard enough sometimes to pray for a few minutes, let alone continually. Anyway, if we were praying continually how would we get anything else done? I am aware of asking these questions for much of my Christian life. Three solutions appear. The first is that life itself is prayer (and prayer, life). I find it harder and harder to see how spirituality and life can be treated separately. They are one. This understanding was undergirded by my second strand – desire – and finds articulation in the third, the Jesus Prayer.

Desire is the motivation for prayer – we desire to be closer to God, desire to be loved, desire to encounter Jesus. It guides us to new ways of praying when the old ways are no longer possible or sustaining. Because love of God has taken hold of us we long to stay within that love and respond to it. Desire grows in us. It actually feeds itself so that the desire creates a longing which cannot ever fully be satisfied in this life but, catching a glimpse of fulfilment, the desire goes deeper and features larger in our lives. I was encouraged many years ago when I read some words of St Augustine,

> Desire itself is your prayer, and if your desire is continuous your prayer is unceasing. For the apostle did not say in vain: Pray without ceasing.
>
> Is it possible that we should unceasingly bend the knee or prostrate our body or raise up our hands that he should tell us: Pray without ceasing?
>
> Or if we say that we pray in this manner I do not think that we are able to do it unceasingly. There is another prayer that is unceasing and interior, and it is desire.
>
> Whatever else you do, if you desire that Sabbath (namely, eternal life) you do not cease to pray. If you do not wish to stop praying, do not stop desiring. Your unceasing desire is your uninterrupted voice. You will grow silent if you stop loving.[1]

This is the second strand of continual prayer – the awareness deep within of a desire for God. Although life is complex and our motives often multi-layered if, at the heart of us, there is a desire for God which is allowed to grow then our prayer will be unceasing. The Jesus Prayer doesn't, I think, make this happen. It simply, gloriously, gives it voice.

But more, this prayer which arises in us unexpectedly points to that greater desire which God has for us. This God of ours longs for us with a desire which is volcanic in power but emerges in gentleness. His desire springs from within his heart and is experienced within our own heart as a longing – maybe a longing which cannot find words – a longing for what we truly are, a longing to be one with the universe and with its creator. As I reflect I realise that the Jesus Prayer often emerges from this deep-felt longing. It is another of God's ways of calling me home.

The Jesus Prayer is, then, my third strand because the Jesus Prayer has enabled me to allow that desire to emerge in the midst of what has been at times a traumatic and unsteady path. It returns to me and draws me back to the encounter with Jesus when I may have wandered far away. It is a home-coming prayer, a joy, a delight.

Desire

As we have seen, some of my earliest memories of passages of Scripture that have touched me have been ones struck through with desire – the desire for God expressed, for example, in Psalm 42, or to see his face in Psalm 27. This insistence by Augustine that desire itself is the secret of continual prayer therefore makes great sense to me. I believe we are drawn to God not by our efforts nor by our prayer but by the realisation of this desire. As the desire burns in us, we naturally pray and we naturally want to live for God.

This desire is a desire of the heart. It is often hidden from our perception. At times it may burn fervently. At other times it is beyond our feeling and our prayer may feel dry and arid. It is still there. A hymn expresses beautifully the need to keep desire alive:

> O thou who camest from above
> The fire celestial to impart,
> Kindle a flame of sacred love
> On the mean altar of my heart.

> There let it for thy glory burn
> With inextinguishable blaze,
> And trembling to its source return
> In humble prayer and fervent praise.

It is itself a reflection on Leviticus 6, where the injunction is to keep the fire burning on the altar. But a fire does not have to blaze to keep going. It may merely smoulder until fresh air gives it new life. So it is with desire. It may only be a tiny flame, no more than a wish that our desire was stronger – but the smallest desire, given light and air, grows and our attraction to God increases.

What I have also discovered is that this desire for God often brings us into struggle as we seek to follow it. This was illustrated beautifully for me on a long retreat. I was to spend thirty days in silence and we were advised to take some craft – something to do whilst we were there. For some reason I opted to take some canvas and some threads. I had never before attempted tapestry and I have not done so since. For these thirty days, though, I stitched away. I let the tapestry record my spiritual journey.

At one point in the retreat I was very aware of God's desire for me and mine for him. Across the top of the tapestry there are therefore various representations of the two desires entwining and bearing fruit. The fruit was portrayed as the pearl of great price, a 'host' – the Eucharist, and a ring representing a lifelong commitment.

What was stunning, on my return, was people's reaction to these two lines of colour which wove together representing these desires. As they met there was the pearl of great price held between the two lines. Almost everybody who saw the tapestry mentioned a snake – something I had to struggle to see but, yes, where the two lines held the pearl it looked like the head of a snake – that symbol of that-which-is-not-God.

It had not been my intention or meaning to suggest that desire brought the snake into play but I know the reality is that when my desire for God is most clear I am also most vulnerable to struggle – in myself and in my life. It is almost as though I am tied up in myself by myriad 'ifs' and 'oughts' – like having a ball of snakes holding me from life. Against them, I know Christ who attracts me to life and draws me away from that which constrains me. The Jesus Prayer not only reveals my desire, expressing it fondly and quietly, it also anchors me in Christ. In the face of my own worst fears and those voices which draw me away from God and from God's love the Jesus Prayer gently calls me back. It is in Jesus that I find my life, my meaning, my purpose – the one who fulfils my heart's desire. In that union with Christ so much else falls away as rubbish (Philippians 3:8) and I am left with desire and a greater freedom.

Heart

In all of this I am aware of the importance of the heart. What I understand as 'heart' is that place in us which God has made for himself – a place where we may wholly respond to him. It is in the heart, in the space of response and encounter, that the Jesus Prayer prays through the silent hours and the storms and passions of our life. It is in the heart that it reminds us of Jesus and calls on his name and his power of humble grace.

It is by praying in the heart that the Jesus Prayer draws us away from reacting thoughtlessly to the present imperatives on our lives and to ponder the deeper calling and meaning of life.

So, in prayer, I find myself taking time to enter my 'heart-space'. It means actually taking care about the position I take for my time of prayer. It's as basic as choosing a seat or cushion which allows me to sit comfortably and alert for the period of prayer. Then it is a question of finding outer stillness as far as possible – turning off the mobile phone and unplugging the landline. It also affects *when* I pray. I have always found that early morning is the best time for me – not only am I more alert but when the children were small it was the only time that the house was quiet.

Outer silence, though, is only the beginning. Then I desire inner silence – a slowing down of my being so that I may attend to God. To slow down I may listen to my breathing or gently repeat a few words, slowly and deliberately – Lord Jesus Christ, Lord Jesus Christ . . .

After a while silence descends and I can enter my heart-space – where it may be possible to encounter the God who comes, longing to make himself known. Often it is the Jesus Prayer or just the name of Jesus that brings me to this place. I cannot make it happen and when it does I often find myself in tears – tears that I record in my journal 'that mingle sadness, love, repentance, tenderness, forgiveness, joy, hope, beauty . . .'

Jesus

Above all, the prayer calls us back to Jesus and to our heart relationship with him. It calls on his name – with all that lies behind the
name – the nature of the Father seen in him, the dynamic, Paschal,
transforming spirit which raised him from death and us to life. By
calling on that name we are aligning ourselves with God's transformation of creation, the bringing in of the Kingdom, not just in us
but through us for others and for the world.

And it is in him that we find our deepest desire.

Certainly this is what I have come to realise as crucial to my own
spiritual journey. I have constantly to remind myself to let go of the
pressing issues of my life and seek an encounter with the living
Lord. In that encounter life is seen in a different perspective.
Without that encounter with this Jesus of tenderness and humility,
there is often little movement or clearer understanding.

The Jesus Prayer reminds me that Jesus is the centre of my life,
the love of my life, the desire of my heart.

And it draws me to Eucharist, for this prayer of beautiful simplicity and profound breadth draws me to the same Jesus I meet in
people and in the sacrament. After celebrating Eucharist with a
team of colleagues I found myself stunned by what I had taken part
in. In a sense this poem also captures the meaning of the Jesus
Prayer for me – it somehow connects prayer and life. It enfleshes
belief.

> Embodiment:
> hands holding
> Body.
> Body holding me.
> Eucharist
> Embodiment.
> All I have waited for,
> longed for
> come to me
> and taken hold of me.
> Restoration
> Embodiment
> Body
> of Christ.

Team assembled
Body gathered
Body holding me
Eucharist
Embodiment.

Resurrection joy
hands burning with delight
holding Body.
Being held.
Healed,
   restored,
      enlivened,
consumed,
   empowered
      abandoned
   affirmed
held and holding
Body
Christ
Jesus.

Praying the Jesus Prayer

Praying the Jesus Prayer could not be simpler – we make a few minutes either end of the day and, settling into the presence of God, meditatively repeat the words calling on Jesus. We may remind ourselves to use it at other times – whenever there is time and when our attention is not needed directly on other things. I have found ironing, gardening, peeling vegetables, washing up, walking and swimming ideal times to practise saying the prayer. In fact, I learnt to swim using the Jesus Prayer. At thirty-five I still could not swim, so, embarrassed and amongst a group of twenty women, I went to classes. Fondly clinging to the side I still found it difficult to trust the water. I discovered I could do it if I didn't think too much about it – so learnt to swim by focusing on the Jesus Prayer. Thus relaxed, my body floated. I am not sure it is a recommended way of learning to swim or saying the Jesus Prayer but it worked for me. What this makes clear is that the Jesus Prayer is not an esoteric practice reserved for monks on Mount Athos but a prayer for ordinary people in everyday life.

In the Orthodox tradition the other aid to saying the prayer is a kind of rosary – but rather than beads there is a series of knots in a rope of fibre. At each recitation the fingers move to the next knot and so the entire body is involved – there is the physical movement of the hands, and the saying of the prayer first with the lips, then by the mind and gradually in the heart . . . it's very akin here to *Lectio Divina* – a drawing of words into wordlessness so that we may encounter Word, may meet Jesus.

It also draws us to deep silence, which we explore next.

Chapter 6

SILENCE

I MUST HAVE BEEN ABOUT THIRTEEN WHEN, eating breakfast, I realised that by collecting coupons from the cereal packet I could get a copy of Paul Simon's 'Sound of Silence'. It was a song that already intrigued me and soon enough the record came – one of those records that stay in the mind and imagination:

> Hello darkness, my old friend,
> I've come to talk with you again,
> Because a vision softly creeping,
> Left its seeds while I was sleeping,
> And the vision that was planted in my brain
> Still remains
> Within the sound of silence.

It would be easy to read too much into my affinity for the song but my reflective nature was already strong. I remember bringing a report home from school feeling really pleased. It wasn't the results that pleased me – it was the comments from one of the teachers. He said two things with amazing clarity and perception, though I am not sure I was supposed to see them as congratulatory. When I was fourteen he wrote, 'Disappointing. He is so quiet that it is difficult to be sure whether or not he is doing his best.' By the time I was seventeen he had seen something more: 'Although quiet by nature, Ivan thinks and feels deeply, and has brought himself to speak up for what he believes.' At last someone saw that the silence was not wilful or aggressive – simply a way of being which I had found creative. I needed silence like other boys (it was an all-boys school) needed sport.

Even now, and as someone who talks in public for a living, I am happier with silence.

> Silence,
> seduces me,
> draws me
> once more
> into abyss of self
> and love
> and GOD.
>
> Silence
> seduces me.
> Let me hear its gentle voice
> let it pierce me
> with its stillness
> embrace me in tranquillity
> the inner certainty of GOD.
> Silence,
> seduces me
> and I have been seduced.

There are many faces of silence – and some of them are friendly

Of course there are many faces of silence and only some of them are friendly. It took me a while to work that out. I guess early in life silence had not only introduced me to God but became too a hiding place – a place where I did not have to say those things which I found it impossible to say – not just physically but emotionally.

I grew up in a family where I was the only one who regularly went to church for most of my teenage years. I was also different in other ways – I seemed bent on a more academic life than my sisters and brother, I liked very different music, even classical, and I had begun to read avidly. Silence, which had so long been my friend, also became a place of isolation. Quite simply there were things I could or would not say to family or friends and so, eventually, to myself. Later, in my thirties, when I was going through immense pain as I cared for Jackie and the children as she declined through Motor Neurone Disease, the pain became too great and my silence needed to be shattered. The pain somehow broke 'the shell of my self understanding'[1] and, over the next ten years after Jackie's death, led me through a deep depression and on to new beginnings. When Paul Simon writes,

> 'Fools' said I, 'You do not know
> Silence like a cancer grows.
> Hear my words that I might teach you,
> Take my arms that I might reach you'

I have an inkling what he means.

Yet if I have misused silence, I am not afraid of it. I have just become more discerning. I recognise that silence, like the whole of life, is capable of being a place of growth and nurture or can be open to other forces.

Certainly it continues, even through the depression, to have been a place of prayer. Deep within me there is a well of silence where God dwells and in that well of silence I find a home.

> And this was the shock,
> this time
> when he walked the barren beach
> with crashing waves
> and rain, heavy wind
> this time
> as he trudged the empty landscape
> – and was it outside or within? –
> there was an inner hospitality
> a conversation of his soul
> with God.
>
> Quiet surprise.
> Wonder.
> It had not been like this before,
> or had it?
> This inner flow of love
> had come by stealth.
> Not chance, not demand . . .
> the daily prayer of forty years
> the plodding prayer through anguish

the questioning of bewilderment
so many times
the crying of grief
but all prayer
all turning to God
and now this
this inner home
where prayer goes on
almost without him
and yet within.
Welcome gift,
if only passing.
Welcome.

Indeed, silence has been the place of my healing. I have found
people to talk through so much of my life – friends, spiritual directors and counsellors – but as they have helped me open my life out,
like that napkin on my lap, I have turned again to the deep place
within, to the silence of divine love, and found healing.

Lord, I love you.
It comes from this deepest place,
   a space carved out by suffering
cathedral-like spaciousness,
   filled with silent praise.

Home again, so long away.
Too long the darkness has submerged me.
Lost in agony of numbness,
I have wandered, touching pain,
   and fleeing, have found it hitting me again –
thrown about,
   slammed by thuggish fears
into steel lockers of hidden memories.

The doors have opened now,
   the memories allowed to breathe,
      the fears subside,
and love has entered silently,
   wanting not to disturb,

only strengthen, release, nurture –
silent music to my soul
   and very life in all my being.

Lord, I love you.

It comes from the deepest place –
the place that you have made for you, in me,
in love.

This poem hints at the healing that silence can bring, but also at its challenges. Maria Boulding writes, 'Our desert place is any place where we confront God. It is the place of truth but also of tenderness.'[2] For me, the silence of God is such a place – the place of truth and tenderness. This silence of God is a silence I find within myself – sometimes only for a few seconds. I recognise it easily. It's like coming home, it's like being wholly me and wholly open and generous to others and to God. It is the silence of the heart.

A place of truth

In that silence, falsehood falters and idols are smashed. If I try to kid myself, if I try to delude myself, the silence simply evaporates. In this place only truth will do. The truth may not be, is unlikely to be, wholly objective truth. It may only be the truth as far as I am able at that time to perceive it but it is *at least* that. As I sit with God in silence this truth is explored, developed and challenged, so that sometimes I find that some idea or way of living that I have held dear has, like an idol, to be smashed. More often I find, however, that they are not so much smashed as dissolved in the light of a clearer and more life-giving truth. All this happens in the place of silence, where God is given free rein in my thoughts and feelings, where God opens me up to a greater vision of himself and of life.

It is not only the place of truth but also of tenderness. Such tenderness is hard to articulate. At times it has been like having Jesus put an arm around my shoulder and just be there. At other times it is a sense of inner life and energy embracing me and bringing me to life – yet coming, not from me, but from the God I have encountered. It is always affirming and strengthening.

It is a paradox that this silence is the place both where I am broken down and built up – as I have written elsewhere 'it tears me to pieces and makes me whole'. How odd that this silence is the place where my worst fears are brought to light and ask to be faced. Yet that, I think, is the way that God works. He reveals his love and invites us to walk into it. Walking into the love of God is walking into a transforming fire – and the consummation of fears and falsehood is a scorching experience.

One of the images I find helpful is from the writings of St John of the Cross.[3]

He suggests that when you watch a log burn it splutters and glows fiercely for a while. It may creak and screech as the fire takes hold. Then it becomes a part of the fire. It is the fire. Here is an image of how we become one with God. Yet somehow in that oneness we also retain our uniqueness.

So, in being approached by pure love we may find that much of us is exposed and needs to be refined and transformed. God will do that transforming work to bring us to a greater knowledge of love. We will become one with him and yet, at the same time, become fully human.

Silence is often the place where such work happens. It is the place of transfiguration where the dross of our life becomes the stuff of eternity. This healing dynamic is at the heart of our relationship with God, or perhaps it is truer to say, at the heart of God's chosen relationship with us. It is the Paschal dynamic, which led Jesus through his passion and death and through the depths of Holy Saturday into Easter life. That same dynamic is at work in us. It is the means by which God draws us to himself. It is a dynamic that is at work not only in our relationship with God but with each other.

God is a friend of silence

In my early years as a Christian one of the people who influenced me most, by her writing and lifestyle, was Mother Teresa of Calcutta. I may not agree with all of her opinions but I certainly responded to her radical discipleship and her abandonment to God.

Many of her words feel written into my soul. Often simple, they nevertheless carry profound meaning. Some such words were, 'God is a friend of silence'. I must have read them hundreds of times and can still remember the book and place on the page where they are written.

God *is* a friend of silence and it is in silence that we may befriend God, ourselves and others. This befriending ourselves is this facing up to our fears and falsehood and coming to terms, as far as we see it, with our reality. Befriending God is God's activity in us as he draws us to himself.

What is less spoken of and yet seems to me to be a crucial part of silence is that in silence we befriend others.

What do I mean?

As I write this I am sitting miles from anyone I know well. I am on retreat in Wales. Yet over these last few days of silence many people have been very close to me. I have rehearsed and played over many relationships, seeking to understand them better. In fact, the same process goes on as for understanding myself – there has to be a breaking down of images so that new ones can emerge.

So often we categorise people, thinking of them in a certain way and relating our relationship with them in familiar patterns. In that way we feel in control of explaining that relationship – but if we let go of these set patterns (idols) we may find that in the silence and love of God we come to a new understanding and so find better ways of relating. I have experienced this time and again in silence.

Perhaps an example or two will help explain this. One person for whom I developed a very different understanding through prayer was my father. In childhood I had a passable but not close relationship with him. When this came up on retreat I could not at first understand why I needed to pray about it, but over a course of some days realised that there were aspects of that relationship which troubled me and which were affecting the way I related to other members of the family as well as to myself. In my prayer I began to look at him not as my father but as a person with his own life history. As I played his life over in my mind and heart (he had died some years earlier) I came to understand him as another person. I felt in touch with him as an individual. I was stunned during my prayer by one particular insight about him for which I had no factual evidence.

When I returned home I made time with my mother to talk about him some more. In that conversation my insight was confirmed and some of the distance I had always felt between my father and me was immediately explained *and overcome*. In my prayer I could now thank God for the relationship that had been.

On another retreat I found a friend coming to mind. Peter had died in his forties and our friendship had therefore come to an abrupt and unexpected end. I thought that I had grieved his loss but in the silence of prayer realised that there were many things I wish I could have said to him. Then I realised that I could say them in the silence to God, asking God who holds Peter in that greater Life to take my words to him.

Both these relationships found an easier place within my inner community of family and friends as a result of these times of prayer, which happened some years ago. But I find the same process happens with current and living friends. Being alone and holding people in the silence of God is a way of deepening friendships despite the distance.

God uses the silence not only to draw us closer to himself, closer to our true selves and closer to other people but also closer to the earth itself. In this way silence becomes our teacher – that teacher which leads us into God's way and so into more abundant life (cf. Isaiah 30).

A place of teaching

Silence is a place where God can teach us. Psalm 51:6 reminds us of God's desire for this truth which we have explored: 'You desire truth in the inward being; therefore teach me wisdom in my secret heart.' Another translation (Roman Catholic Breviary) has 'in the stillness of my heart, teach me wisdom'. We might almost say 'In the silence of my heart, teach me', for this silence of God is our unique place of education where God can draw forth wisdom as we reflect with him on our experience.

It is here that Jesus' words, 'They shall all be taught by God' (John 6:45) find their reality. It is here that we hear and learn from the Father. This learning in the heart is our most powerful learning, where we allow God to transform our mind and heart. It is the place where the Paschal dynamic takes root in our thoughts and feelings. But more, this 'learning silence' is not just something which happens between ourselves and God; it happens too in our relationships with other people when we give ourselves to (holy) listening.

In a telling phrase Rubem A. Alves[4] writes, 'Truth lies inside the silence which is around the words,' and he carries on, 'One must pay attention to what is not said, to read between the lines.'

The whole of life then becomes the place of learning as we allow God to speak his truth in the silence surrounding the words and surrounding the events that confront us. To listen well is to learn.

Silence as the place of encounter

Silence, then, can hold all the frenzied fears of isolation or all the joy and hope of solitude. It is the place of encounter. When we stay in silence the surface chatter eventually gives way to deeper resonances – our past, our desires, our hopes. Some of those resonances will give us joy, and others pain.

To enter silence with God is not to be victim to all these resonances but to hold them before God, talking to God about them as one would with a friend. In such silence it is important to be discerning about where thoughts and feelings are coming from. Some will bring us life and to a sense of the presence of God. Others will bring us to a dullness that is not life at all. Reflecting on times of silence we may become aware of times when we were led to encounter something about ourselves that helped us grow in faith, hope and love and other times when we were merely cast into confusion, self-doubt and maybe even self-loathing.

The tradition suggests that we discern these different feelings and then spend more time with those which lead us towards life, love and energy.

Of course, that's not as superficial as it sounds. It's not about staying with the frothy surface but about staying with the deeper attractions – so, for instance, what actually is drawing us to God may be both increasing love and life in us but may also be painful as we encounter areas of our life that have yet to be healed. Equally, what feels immediately good may in the longer term hold nothing for us.

In this discernment of spirits we are reminded of all that was said in Chapter 1 about the need for reflection.

The real delight of silence is when it becomes a place of healing – a place where the fragments of our lives find some wholeness, when our relationships with others find a deeper connection, and our relationship with God reflects that relationship which he created us to have and which we will have in eternity.

In the following chapters we will continue to see how the whole of life becomes the place of awed silence as we encounter God in all that we experience.

Chapter 7

CREATION AND CREATIVITY

GOD CATCHES ME BY SURPRISE. It's often in the most unexpected places and when I am thinking about something altogether different that he makes himself known. As Ian McEwan says of an author in his book *Amsterdam*, 'The best ideas caught him by surprise at the end of twenty miles when his mind was elsewhere.'[1]

So I found myself at the end of a long walk, standing in Llandudno, looking at the mountains. To my mind came some simple yet life-enhancing words, 'Before the mountains were formed I loved you.' I had forgotten all about the experience when, six years on, again by the sea and looking at mountains – this time at Barmouth – another phrase came to mind, 'Before the mountains were formed I made you beautiful for me.'

Where do such words come from – maybe from my own desires and subconscious? I think not – not in the sense that they have their origin there. They come, I believe, from experiencing the joy they bring, from God himself speaking through an accumulated knowledge of Scripture and spiritual reading, through creation itself, through my senses and, yes, even through my subconscious. That validates rather than invalidates them because they are signs of God using all he has made to communicate with his people. What else would he do? An incarnate God uses our humanity to reveal his Word. Grace builds on nature to perfect it.

It's as though all that surrounds us enters into a dialogue in our soul to draw us closer to God. Having looked at the mountains I return again to Ephesians 1:4: '. . . as he chose us in Christ before the foundation of the world to be holy and blameless before him in love.' Indeed, in Christ we share something of the glory he had with the Father before the world existed (John 17:5). We may be made from dust, but we are dust to be glorified – as the Eastern Orthodox tradition would remind us, we are to be become more and more like God, a process which is neatly summed up by the word 'christification' – being transformed more and more into Christ's likeness.

So, in a few short steps of reflection on some mountains, I am drawn to my desire and goal in life – that for which God created each of us – to find union with him.

Creation holds this power – it is God's Word waiting to be heard with its own wisdom and insight into the creator – a constant source of prayer.

From mountains to butterflies

Every part of creation may speak to us in this way. One day it may be mountains rising through the reddened mist of a golden sunrise. On another it may be as simple as a butterfly.

For a period of two years butterflies became incredibly significant in my spiritual life. It was as though they were messengers of God. They somehow spoke of God's intimacy at a time when little else was reaching me. On one occasion, as I led a Eucharist, a butterfly emerged out of a church's gloom and landed on my vestments. Immediately my heart and soul were lifted to God.

Then, over a period of three days, a number of incidents happened which surely have a natural explanation but which also had, for me, amazing and powerful significance. An elderly friend died at a time when she was ready to go, shortly after Christmas one year. The church, kept at a reasonable temperature, obviously gave the butterflies a safe wintering place. On 6 January I wrote:

> A butterfly
> alighted on my hand –
> Epiphany
> and Mass.
> In simple trust
> it stayed there
> on my hand
> and spoke to me
> of my friend.
> As my mind
> saw her land

in trust
in God
so the butterfly
flew up
and
disappeared
in the Chapel's gloom,
and I knew, *I knew*,
my friend
too had flown
into heaven's light.

Later I saw
a butterfly
dead.
I felt no sadness
How could I?
She is not here.
She is risen. Alleluia.

That might have been it, and it would have been enough. The night
before the funeral, however, we brought the coffin into church at the
time of Evensong. The butterfly joined us:

Butterfly,
symbol of immortality,
of resurrection life
beyond
the
waters of death
I praise you.

There you were,
joining our Vespers' prayer.
Still,
contemplative
before your maker,
a reminder of our heart's
desire and stand.
How I enjoyed you.

Butterfly or angel,
how can I discern?
You certainly were
a messenger
and took my heart to God.
You reminded me that
she whom we love
is in his keeping.

Fly then butterfly,
to join the angels' choir,
and use your heavenly voice
to sing our praise to God.
Fly, let your beauty ascend into
heaven's realm
and catch the Father's eye
as you caught mine.
May your beauty be our thanks.

The following day we held a Requiem. When we came to the Peace
I went to shake someone's hands. Imagine my amazement to see
that on those hands rested a butterfly. It was the prefect way to
remember my friend.

Where else would it be
but in a hand
of peace?

My friend
may you
rest in peace
and rise
with butterflies abundant,
myriad colours,
in glory.
Amen.

But the butterflies had not finished and what followed left me
stunned. I have yet to find adequate words to describe it. In all my
years of ministry nothing else like it has happened. There, as we

celebrated the Eucharist, when the chalice was momentarily uncov-
ered, a butterfly flew out of the roof down towards the altar. I
watched, transfixed. The butterfly flew down and into the chalice
before I could cover it. It swooped into the chalice and then flew out
again – just a little wine falling from its wings. Here was an image
of dying and rising that burnt itself into my very being. In that
momentary event baptism, life, the Eucharist and my friend's life
and death came together.

It bears out the poem by Franz Kafka:

> You do not have to leave the room.
> Remain standing in your place and listen.
> Do not even listen, simply wait.
> Do not even wait.
> Be quite still and solitary.
>
> The world will freely offer itself to you
> To be unmasked.
> It has no choice
> It will roll in ecstasy at your feet.[2]

What I have experienced in these and in so many other ways
through the awareness of creation stems from being prepared to
enter solitude and see things with fresh eyes in a wonder of contemplation. It is 'like poets to wrap your solitude around you and
catch your meanings unawares'.[3] It is to listen, as we said in Chapter
6, to the truth which is in the silence around the words, around
what we initially see. This can happen not only with creation itself,
of course, but with everything and everyone around us.

Creativity

Walking one day into a craft centre in Ruthin in Wales I was un-
prepared for what I saw. I imagined quaint pottery perhaps, some
glassware, some watercolours. As I entered the courtyard, however,
my breath was taken away, and I stood and gawped at a statue
which spoke profoundly to me of God. In fact, the sculptor had been
commissioned to create a piece – one of a pair – to stand outside a
local superstore. The one I saw was a father with three children. The
other, I gather, was to be of a woman with a pushchair.

The father was solid, a chunky character, bearded and resolutely gazing whilst he held a small child in his arms. Just behind him, clinging to his leg, was a shy boy peering round his father as he might around a tree. Just behind the father and on the other side was a girl with plaited hair. She was the tease of the family, clutching one of the boy's shoes hidden behind her back. There was a great resonance of love about the sculpture. Somehow each of these three very different children found their love and life in the solidity of the father. There was humour and laughter and a sense that the father cared for these children.

I write that ten years on. That's what it has come to mean to me. But when I first saw it I was devoid of thought. Somehow I was one of those children and the father, God. I was held in awe and silence as I just walked around the sculpture. Coming a bit more to my senses I began to feel myself as each of the children and then as the father. Here was a piece of stone, which had been given a heart of flesh and was speaking to me not by the sculptor's design but by God's inspiration and intent. My reaction was not controlled by the artist or by me. My reaction stemmed from my prayer around that time, in which I was exploring the fatherhood of God in my life. Again, God was using all my senses and my lack of sense to show me that which I could not see by prayer secluded in some religious place. I needed my eyes opened in other ways. That sculpture has stayed with me as a source of inspiration – a friend took photos from every angle for me to gaze at from time to time. Like the butterfly it was another messenger from God.

One of the reasons art and music and poetry so fascinate me is that the artist or musician or poet who is truly creative makes me look and listen to the whole of life with different eyes and ears, so that in the depth of contemplation or, to put it less religiously, when I 'gawp' well, when I listen well, I see, I hear, God.

One such artist is a Canadian, Gathie Falk. Gathie paints and sculpts. One sculpture is of a number of pottery cabbages hanging from the ceiling. The first impression is no more than that – cabbages hanging from a ceiling – but then your eye settles on one cabbage, and then on one leaf or stalk and as you gaze you begin to see just how beautiful a cabbage is. The ordinary gives way to the extraordinary, the natural to the supernatural and from then on every cabbage becomes an icon – a window into God.

Another artist who turns my vision upside down is Stanley

Spencer and especially his paintings of Christ in the wilderness. Each one is based on a verse of Scripture. At times Jesus is obviously at peace, at others he is deep in the struggle of the desert and at others he is childlike, kneeling on all fours, gazing at the lilies of the field. One of the paintings in particular strikes me and moves me deeply, so that I am caught up in its action. In it Jesus is looking at a scorpion which sits on his hand . . . Jesus gazing, Jesus deep in contemplation. Forty days in the wilderness and there he is, stripped to the poverty and the wealth of having nothing at all, and nothing between him and the Father . . . *'a condition of complete simplicity costing not less than everything'.*

Can you imagine him happening on some insect or plant, the way you do when wandering alone, and just being lost in wonder as he marvels at the creation which, like him, is the visible life of the divine Word – that Word which brings all things into being? Can you imagine him lost in reverie, absorbed like a child listening to a seashell . . . listening, watching intently with his soul?

Here in the desert there is little to catch the eye. It is a place of simplicity . . . and a place of struggle with demons and self-will, and it is in the desert that we see them, feel them most clearly, as we might see an insect or a stone clearly against the desert waste. As I gaze at Spencer's picture I am reminded that the scorpion is symbolic of evil, of treachery and of betrayal – a symbol too for Judas Iscariot. In his life Jesus holds all of that before the Father.

There is no other way. The evil spirit will try every which way to draw our attention off God and onto the scorpion or weeds of our lives so that we do not see beyond ourselves to the Father. We cannot afford to give him space. Instead we call with our lips, have on our heart the one word which for us calls on the mystery which is God, and as we enter the wilderness which is within us we speak that word so that God may speak his Word in us. As we ponder this image we may let everything that we see, hear, think, feel, taste and touch draw us back to the centre of our being, where God dwells. When we are drawn away, let us gently bring ourselves back, gently so that we may hear the faintest whisper of the voice of love and when our gaze is drawn to the areas of our lives which seem to threaten us, we can let go of the fear that leads to shame, and look rather with love, look through to the Father and wait, stay still, until it is *his* time to do what he must do – pour himself out in love that you, that I, might be healed.

And all this from a picture.

If Spencer draws me to confrontation with evil, then another artist draws me to an astounding peace. It is the artist Mark Rothko, whose works simply envelop and embrace me and lead me to a deep place where I encounter God. As I write I am transported to the Tate Modern in London where one room is set aside for his work. Those enormous canvasses of blocks of colour have become an inner resource. I return to the memory of a single visit to that room and find myself in a place of deep peace.

If I allow that room of his paintings to take shape in my imagination it is almost like standing in a vast cathedral at the end of the Eucharistic prayer – a moment caught beautifully by the poet Osip Mandelstam:

> Here is the pyx, like a golden sun,
> For a splendid moment hanging in the air;
> Now only the Greek tongue should resound,
> Holding the whole world in its hands like an apple.
>
> The exultant zenith of the service has come round,
> Light under the dome in the circular temple in July,
> So that with nothing held back we sigh, beyond time,
> For that green pasture where time holds still.
>
> And the Eucharist hovers like an eternal midday –
> All partake, play and sing;
> Under the eyes of everyone the holy vessel pours
> With inexhaustible rejoicing.[4]

Rothko achieves in me a miracle every time I encounter his work. He takes me to this vast place and drops me into God.

All we have to do is look and wait to see what unfolds – what touches each one of us will be different, but to take time to be nourished by art and sculpture is a real act of opening oneself to God speaking through the unexpected.

Being creative ourselves

Against the backdrop of God's artistry and the creativity of some of the great artists we may feel that our own attempts at creativity are futile. Not so.

As someone whose artistic skills are limited I am constantly astounded by what my attempts at art and sculpture teach me about God and about myself. Only recently I led an art workshop to help people get in touch with their deepest desires.

Giving people some paper and a few pastels I invited them to complete, fairly spontaneously, four statements:

- In my relationship with myself I desire . . .
- In my most intimate relationships I desire . . .
- In my relationship with creation I desire . . .
- In my relationship with God I desire . . .

Then I invited them to ponder what deeper desires lay behind these initial ones. To help them discover these deeper desires I suggested they play with colours on the paper and see what emerged. Finally, I asked them to repeat the playing with colours whilst praying for God to show them their deepest desires.

When we came to the end of the exercise we had a strange collection of 'art' – some beautiful, some childish – but each of us had discovered something profound about what we really desired in life. Our creativity was giving God space to speak to us in fresh and illuminating ways.

'Before the mountains were formed I made you beautiful for me' may have been the way God speaks through his own creation. Through my creativity I made a response – my one desire and choice is to give myself to God. Creation and creativity had entered dialogue as they so often do and in the spaces as well as in the words of the dialogue fresh truths emerge.

Chapter 8

MUSIC

IF THERE IS ONE ART FORM which has been consistently used to draw me to God it would be music. Music feeds my soul. It delights my heart and so often speaks to me the things of God. Sometimes it simply transports me to a glimpse of heaven.

Having moved recently to Liverpool I wandered into the Tate Gallery expecting to see the works of art and sculpture there. As I climbed the stairs I began to hear music and entering the upper floor found myself in a room with forty loudspeakers. Each one carried a single voice and together the voices were singing Tallis' 'Spem in alium'. The installation, by the Canadian artist Janet Cardiff, was for me a little piece of heaven on the Mersey. For weeks I sent other people to listen to the music and each came back with the same sense of wonder. If sloth is nothing less than the loss of the sense of wonder then here, in that gallery, was an antidote to sloth. This can be the power of music.

It can thrill and delight us not just in the sense that it has an emotional impact but in the sense that it can change our view of life. It can involve us in a movement of the soul. It can be purposely used as an introduction to prayer. It can, indeed, become prayer. It can be the means by which God speaks to us directly and clearly.

Music can change our view of life

I remember once going to a potentially fraught meeting and deciding at the last moment to begin by playing a piece of music in the room lit only by a candle. The piece of music was by the Estonian composer Arvo Part – a piece called 'Spiegel im Spiegel'. As people listened to the music they calmed down and came to a place of great stillness. In that spacious and delicious calm we found we were able to address contentious issues in a way that was constructive and purposeful and that had long-lasting effects.

Reflecting on that incident I am reminded of the first classical music that really affected me. At the age of fifteen, knowing little about music, I bought a gramophone in a jumble sale. With it I bought a selection of 78s – everything from Mozart to Gracie Fields, from Tchaikovsky to Kathleen Ferrier. Ferrier was singing two songs, 'Art thou troubled, music will calm thee' and 'What is life to me without thee?'

As an introduction to the world of classical music the selection was a little arbitrary but Ferrier's song has almost been a benediction on my life – music has calmed me. Through the joys and traumas of life, music has been my constant companion.

Music can involve us in a movement of the soul

How can the soul respond to God? Reflecting on Scripture one is reminded of the meeting of Mary and Elizabeth. As they meet (Luke 1:39ff) we are told that as Elizabeth heard Mary's greeting the child leapt in her womb. Music, for me, has that capacity. As I encounter God through music, my soul rises within me and brings me to life.

Any kind of music can have this effect – from the music of Thomas Tallis with its haunting and weaving voices, to the music of some of the latest musicians. But what is happening when this leaping of the soul occurs? My own understanding is captured by a poem written several years ago:

> A violin note hangs in the air,
> the string vibrates with life
> though its cause is for
> an instant gone –
> the touch of bow
> the caress that brought life
> no longer, for an instant there
> And that is how I feel . . .[1]

For me music is the touch of God upon my soul – the bow upon my strings. Imagine then my joy when recently I found a quotation from Mechtild of Magdeburg:

> The Holy Spirit is our harpist,
> and all the strings
> which are touched in love
> Must sound.

It is through music that God so often draws me back to himself or deeper into his friendship. It is as if by music that God touches every part of me – often moving me in ways that other stimuli do not reach. Sometimes it may be simply instrumental music. At other times it may be the timbre of a voice or the poetry of words. Sometimes, of course, it is a combination and then I find myself moved most fully.

Recently it happened listening to Eva Cassidy sing a song by Claire Hamill. The song, a love song, became for me an allegory of my love for God. As I listen I am lost in love for God:

> Sometimes it amazes me
> how strong the power of love can be
> sometimes it just takes my breath away.
> You watch my love grow
> like a child
> sometimes genuine, sometimes wild.
> Sometimes you just take my breath away.

> *And it's too good to slip by*
> *too good to lose*
> *too good to be there just to abuse.*
> *I'm gonna stand out on a mountaintop*
> *and tell the news*
> *that you take my breath away.*

> Sometimes it amazes me
> how strong the power of love can be
> sometimes it just takes my breath away.

> Your beauty is there in all I see
> and when I feel your eyes on me
> don't you know you just take my breath away.

> *And it's too good to slip by*
> *too good to lose*

too good to be there just to abuse.
I'm gonna stand out on a mountaintop
and tell the news
that you take my breath away. (Repeat)

O yes, you take my breath away.

Here is a song that not only speaks of love but of a fundamental aspect of my prayer – the belief that God gazes at us with love. This is an attitude with which I come to prayer – very much following the tradition of Ignatius of Loyola, who suggests that before we pray we spend the space of an 'Our Father' considering how God our Lord is looking at us.

This gaze of God is the gaze in which I become who I am, the gaze which enables me to offer myself to others and to God.[2] As I heard the song for the first time my soul leapt within me, recognising Christ through the words. Music indeed moves my soul and takes my breath away.

Music can be purposely used as an introduction to prayer

I must be a slow learner because it took me ages to recognise that God was doing this through music and then to make the connection that if I played the piece of music which had touched me it might lead me into deeper prayer.

Sometimes it is simply finding a piece of music which calms me down – the Arvo Part piece already mentioned or the Samuel Barber 'Adagio for Strings'. At other times, as with Eva Cassidy, it is the words that speak. What is clear to me, however, is that often the pieces that speak most profoundly are not intentionally religious pieces. God speaks through the unexpected.

This has been an important insight and one worth pondering. It began to make sense when I read Sister Wendy Beckett's book, *Art and the Sacred*. In it she differentiates 'spiritual' and 'religious' art, with religious art being that which intentionally depicts a religious theme and spiritual art being that which evokes in us a spiritual response. In the light of the previous chapter it is worth quoting her on Rothko:

The artist may even disavow all spiritual intentions, as Rothko did, annoyed at what he felt were misreadings of his abstractions. But nobody can look at a major Rothko without feeling its spiritual power, being affected by it and also being challenged. It is this challenge, this silent exposure of potential within ourselves, a touch of the infinite, that gives force to Don Cupitt's statement on the Sacred Abstract. It is also why so many people unconsciously fear and resist art. We may not want to become aware of suppressed and unrecognised aspects of ourselves.[3]

For me, music, like art, has this capacity to open us up to fresh truth and when we approach truth with humility I believe we approach the presence of God.

Religious music may do this for us but often it carries layers of meaning which make it opaque and so unlikely to give us fresh spiritual vision. Other music, though, written with completely different motivation may lift us to the heights. Writing this is easy as I listen, in my mind, to a whole range of music that inspires prayer.

Music can indeed become prayer

There are times when the resonance between a piece of music and the soul is so great that the music lifts the soul into the very presence of God. It has then not only played the soul as a person might brush the strings of a harp but the music and the soul become, for a while, one. The music, like a vast wave, lifts the soul and gently lays it on the shore of heaven where an encounter with God is inevitable.

Salisbury Cathedral was twice the setting where this happened for me. The first time was during a service and the singing of Allegri's 'Miserere'. The rest of the service passed me by. I had encountered God and found myself in caverns of stillness where I knew myself infinitely beloved.

On another occasion the cathedral was virtually empty but the organist was practising a piece of music I later came to identify as being by Cesar Franck. It stopped me in my tracks, making me sit down and listen. Again there was the stillness and again the sense of being held in the presence and graciousness of God.

It seems to me that these are not extraordinary occurrences. They happen reasonably often. What changes them into the extraordinary is when I am fully aware and give them attention, when I allow myself to become receptive to the fact that there is more here than an emotional response to what I hear . . . as I become more aware, so the music becomes secondary to the sense of the numinous and beautiful.

And the prayer? The prayer is a prayer of union with God – a meeting of desires where love erupts and grows.

Music can be the means by which God speaks to us directly and clearly

We have seen, at the beginning of Chapter 2, how God has used snippets of songs to speak directly to me and earlier in this chapter how the Eva Cassidy song became for me like the scriptural 'Song of Songs' – a personal love song to God. In this way God has often used music to speak directly to my life situation. Again it requires awareness to realise that God is speaking, it requires space to listen to the deeper meanings and it requires discernment to ensure, as far as we are able, that what we hear is indeed from God.

Awareness lies at the heart of so much prayer. It is awareness that makes us use all our senses: first to appreciate what God is doing for us and then to respond.

In the 'Contemplatio' at the end of the Ignatian *Spiritual Exercises*, we are drawn to realise just how God reveals his love to us – a love that shows itself in deeds as well as words and which is mutual. As a response to that love we are invited to pray Ignatius' beautiful prayer of abandonment:

> Take, Lord, and receive
> all my liberty,
> my memory,
> my understanding,
> and my entire will –
> all that I have and call my own.
> You have given it all to me.
> To you, Lord, I return it.
> Everything is yours;
> do with it what you will.
> Give me only your
> LOVE and your GRACE.
> That is enough for me.

I quote the prayer simply because it came to mind as a result of hearing a piece of music. I had gone to see the film *Master and Commander*. During the film, set on the high seas, the captain and ship's doctor relax by playing music. As they played part of Corelli's *Christmas Concerto* I found myself wrapped in love, and moved by it I took the music into my prayer the next morning. Wrapped in the love I had experienced in the film I found myself wanting to respond with the whole of my being. It was then that Ignatius' prayer came to mind as the only response to a consuming sense of innate abandoned love – God's love set free in me. I doubt that the makers of the film imagined that their choice of music would affect a middle-aged vicar living in Liverpool, but God uses everything in his creation, everything, to help us to know him so that we might, again to quote Ignatius, reverence and serve him.

Awareness, then, can be a key. But, as has been said, the awareness needs space so that we can listen to the deeper meaning. Had I just been moved by the music and by the love it would have been enough, but the experience of taking that music into prayer has taken a simple moment and turned it into something more lasting – a moment in eternity. It is simply a matter of allowing what has touched the mind or emotions to touch that place in us which God has made for himself – the heart where we are continually being transformed into the likeness of Christ.

Otherwise, to quote that wonderful phrase from T. S. Eliot, we have the experience but miss the meaning. Giving space to what touches us allows us to savour the meaning and enjoy the full depth of what has sparked us into life.

It means that we enter the many layers of meaning that, particularly, a piece of music may have for us. As I write I am playing the *Christmas Concerto*. It evokes all sorts of memories of Christmases past, but also of a particular group of young musicians who have been an inspiration throughout the last twenty years.[4] I suppose it was these youngsters who taught me that God resides in beauty. He cannot help himself but speak forth from that which is beautiful and tender and true. Listening to these gifted musicians brings me to the tears of encounter and joy that I know to be God's gift.[5]

Listening to these musicians also taught me much about what it means to give everything to that which is wanting to emerge in us – our true self with all its multi-faceted and abundant gifts. They taught me how discipline, rightly understood, gives freedom.

As I listen to the music and as I pray all these memories come back and speak to my situation now as I seek to give myself to God in new and risky living – and all this because of a few bars of music in a seafaring adventure. This is, for me, how God is – using the ordinary events of life to reveal the secrets of heaven. Everything can be alive with God.

This awareness also requires discernment to ensure, as far as possible, that what we hear is indeed from God. If music can move us powerfully towards God and his dream for us, it can also move us to melancholy and despair. It can evoke memories and situations that are destructive in our lives. Discernment is essential. If music is taking us away from life, then it is best not to listen to that particular music. It almost seems too obvious to say and yet in a culture where music may be no more than wallpaper we can find ourselves listening to much that would not be our choice.

If we find ourselves listening to music that stirs up our emotions we may need first to give it space – to take it into prayer and then discern whether it is opening up the pain that is healing or the pain that simply drains us of energy and motivation, that mocks our humanity and worth. As always, the question is whether it draws us to consolation (with the sun, closer to God) or desolation (without the sun, away from God).

What is important is that we give space to listen to our reaction and then to discern, so that, if we have been profoundly moved, we may use the experience for our growth and healing.

Feeding the soul

Music, as is apparent, feeds my soul. It has been, and continues to be, the means by which God sustains me through the darkest parts of my journey (the pop group Queen saw me through Jackie's death, for example) and on the lighter parts has provided not only nourishment but sheer delight and joy.

It is such a gift and yet we may listen to it so casually that we fail to hear the deeper resonances and don't allow it to be a vehicle of that dynamic and life-giving Spirit of God. Music is, in many ways, a sacrament for me – a means of God's grace not visible but audible – God using our senses to reach us with himself.

Chapter 9

EUCHARIST

WHEN THE CHURCH OF ENGLAND PERMITTED THE ORDINATION OF WOMEN I was delighted to be invited to lead the ordination retreat in the Diocese of St Edmundsbury and Ipswich. It was a retreat that still burns in my memory. To echo the previous chapter, music played a significant part. As these women had waited to be accepted for ordination (and some of them had known themselves called to priesthood for many years) so the people of South Africa had waited for the end of apartheid. As the retreat went on I was very much aware of the media images of the very long queues of South Africans waiting to vote.

During the retreat we found ourselves singing many of the South African freedom songs. Even as we prepared to enter the cathedral we sang gently and quietly 'Thumi mina' and the more lively 'We are marching'.

As I prepared my talks for the retreat I reflected on the Eucharist afresh. I wondered how it would feel for them, after so much waiting, to take bread and wine for the first time and say, 'This is my body' . . . 'This is my blood.'

On the wall of the retreat house was a poster. It was the intersection of fences at the corner of four fields. In each field the animal was straining its head through the fence wires to eat the grass in the next field. The words were simply, 'The grass is greener . . .' I wondered whether, having entered the field of 'priesthood' there would be joy or disappointment, whether the grass was really greener when one became a priest. I remember reading Veronica Zundel's poem, 'The Late Bride':

> And so she finally
> after all those years

opened the box.
And out flew
nothing.
And was that all, she cried
there was in it?
Then why did I dream and yearn
scrabble and fight so long
to get my hands on it?

That was at first
it was only later she learnt,
slowly, so slowly
to fill the box with
the treasures she had
unknowing, owned all along.[1]

I realised the truth of the poem for these ordinands. They were already people of great gifting. God would draw out of them all that he needed them to be.

But what of celebrating the Eucharist? Would that fall flat – nothing flying out when the box was opened? It made me reflect on how the Eucharist has been for me – as someone who receives, as someone who presides and as someone who prays.

That was several years ago now and I remember hoping that what I felt then – that the Eucharist was still an enormous privilege and gift – would carry on however long I lived. It has. It still burns my hands, sometimes, to hold the bread and wine, whether I am receiving or presiding. It still moves me to tears and fills me with love.

Someone who receives

Of course, at times it is just part of a routine, but the Eucharist has often been far more than routine – far more like the burning bush – a means by which God calls me. If I look back I realise that the first time it had this meaning for me was on a Norfolk beach. The youth group to which I belonged was having a camping holiday and we had the Eucharist there on the beach.

Somehow it made it all the more meaningful. It was not difficult to imagine the first disciples sharing a meal with Jesus, or to imagine ourselves as part of the same company.

There have been other times when the host held before me has simply touched my very being into life. One particular instance springs to mind – a time when I was on retreat.

The day finished with half an hour of silent prayer before the Blessed Sacrament. As I gazed on it I found myself seeing not a piece of bread but a baby and in my imagination it was clear that the baby was me held in the love of God. This baby was deeply significant for it represented the 'me' that I tend, in my care for others, to ignore at everyone's peril. To know myself held in the love of God is the only true place I can make sound judgements, the only place from where I best serve other people, the only place from where I can truly offer my whole self to God. This moment on retreat was therefore deeply significant. It was later that I wrote:

> As a baby lies
> ensconced within a mother's love
> so am I before you,
> my loving God.
> All I am derives from you,
> my body sanctified by yours,
> my heart quickened by your love,
> my thoughts kindled
> by your gift of reason.
> All I am derives from you,
> and I, overwhelmed by love
> would surrender all to you.
>
> As a lover lies,
> in simple joy in the beloved's arms
> so do I lie in you,
> my 'lover' God
> – all I am made holy by your clasp,
> all I am dignified by your presence
> transfigured, by your touch, into joy,
> and I, overwhelmed by love
> would surrender all to you.

Everything I am and have
is yours, Lord –
your gift of me to me.
I offer now this gift,
wanting nothing in return,
wanting only to offer love to love,
to surrender all to you –
to place myself in your embrace
that you may take this gift
of me to you
and, blessing it,
use all to your praise and glory.
Amen.

But there have been other times when simply receiving communion
has completely turned me upside down, making me aware of God's
love in a way that little else can do. I heartily endorse Christopher
Nolan's comment that 'God assumed beautiful credit by breathing
love through the Eucharist.'[2]

There have been extended periods in my life when even as a
priest I have presided seldom at the communion table – for the
three years that I looked after my wife full time and more recently
as I work in a Roman Catholic retreat house.

These times have been important experiences of knowing the
Eucharist as one who receives more often than one who presides. It
draws me to the conclusion that receiving is the central act.
Receiving the sacrament is the point of infinite silence where the
world stops and we are linked with God, and with all God's people
on earth and heaven. Indeed, the first time I presided after Jackie
died the words 'with angels and archangels and with all the company of heaven' burnt into me. In communion I am linked with all
I love.

Someone who presides

The poems in Chapter 5[3] and Chapter 13[4] speak profoundly of how
it feels to preside at a Eucharist. Over twenty-five years it has
gained rather than lessened in significance, in a sense of privilege
and in an awe which is way beyond any words. There are occasions
when it continues to simply take my breath away.

The circumstances and place seem to have little impact – whether one is presiding in a vast church or in a home. For me it always demands a sense of respect. Here, indeed, is holy ground. It is here, when one stands at the altar, that life and meaning find their greatest focus. And who am I in this great moment? All I am is the hands of the gathered assembly of God's people. I am not there simply as me but as the one who is privileged to say the words and do the actions that the people of God wish to do.

This sense of the Eucharist being an act that all take part in is deeply important to me. I am not worthy to claim any special part or any great holiness. Indeed, I am more aware of my lack of holiness now than when I was first ordained. If it depended on merit I would not be there. The same, of course, may be true of all those gathered. I doubt any are perfect. But we are graced. We are graced to do these things with Christ being the host. It is Christ who is the one who celebrates Eucharist for us, through us and in us.

He celebrates for us. When I remember that Eucharist on the beach at Eccles in Norfolk I am also drawn to those incidents in John's gospel where the risen Christ eats with the disciples on the beach. There is a real sense that it is the same Christ who was on the Eccles beach and who is present in every Eucharist.

He celebrates through us. If it is Jesus who celebrates then he celebrates through the gathered church – the Body of Christ in that place. In that sense, even when I am receiving rather than presiding, I am still playing an active part in celebrating the Eucharist. As one of the group who have met I am necessarily involved in the celebration of the Eucharist.

He celebrates in us. When we receive the bread and wine, the Body and Blood, Eucharist becomes us. As St Augustine said of our place in receiving communion: 'Receive what you are, for you are with him in the bread, you are with him in the chalice.' We are the Body of Christ receiving the Body of Christ. In the receiving we not only affirm what we are but open ourselves to that transforming dynamic where we become more than we already are – more and more being released into the likeness of Christ. So why do I not feel more holy? I guess because being transformed more and more into Christ is being drawn more and more into truth and into the recognition that it does not depend on me but on grace.

Being drawn into truth has become, for me, an important aspect of the Eucharist. When I offer communion to others what am I doing except offering the truth of Jesus to the truth of their life. Often, then, as I preside and go along the communion rail I am very aware of people's life circumstances. Saying, 'The Body of Christ' to first a single mum, and then a bereaved widow, then perhaps to a newly confirmed teenager . . . each time I am offering the truth of Jesus to individual and unique people. I pray that the truth of Jesus will bless and transform their truth . . . that it will bless and transform mine.

It is often this sense of the reality of what I am doing when I preside, which fills me with immense awe and leads me to a necessary silence and sometimes to tears.

It is here
here
when I hold you
my loving Christ
in simple bread.
Here that I know
deep down
your truth
your reality
your presence.

Here
that I feel
most empty
of me.
Only you matter.
Let me become
invisible
transparent
to your presence.

And yet
here
that I am
most truly alive
true to myself
true to you.

Lord, I love you
this deep down love
emerges
here in the silence
of our meeting
your body
mine
embracing
each other.

Respect, love
honour, obey
trust, hope
fulfilment
joy.
You,
only you
in love
with each and all
as in my hands
I offer you
to those who come
the body . . . the blood . . .
the living one
you immobile
in a piece of bread,
dynamic in their hearts.

Someone who prays

So the Eucharist is at the heart of my prayer – both as someone who receives and as someone who presides. It is the touchstone of my prayer even when I feel nothing, hear nothing, see nothing, and that is my most common experience at the Eucharist. I know that it is crucial to my well-being that I attend and that I allow myself to be open.

In terms of the context of my prayer life I guess the Eucharist is above all about relationship. Even when it feels that I am going out of habit, with no particular sense of presence, it still draws me – as much as it is important in any committed relationship to affirm love even when the feelings are running dry.

That committed relationship is about self-giving. Again it was when on retreat that I received communion from a sister. As she gave me the bread I guess she said 'The Body of Christ' but what I heard in my inner being was 'With my body I honour you, all that I am I give to you, and all that I have I share with you' – words from the then current marriage service. I remember smiling a broad smile. She probably thought I was completely off-the-wall. But those words have stayed with me and sometimes come back as I receive communion. What is Christ doing except honouring us with his body, giving us all that he is and sharing all that he has? It is another of those moments of truth – like the one in Luke 24, where the two on the Emmaus road suddenly realise who Jesus is and what he is offering.

For me, though I believe Jesus to be making this commitment all the time, the Eucharist somehow acts as a clear and unambiguous sacrament of relationship. When I am drawn to fall away the Eucharist brings me back. It is enough to be present and to let our 'Yes' to God meet and engage with God's 'Yes' to us.

For me that happened most profoundly on a thirty-day retreat – the kind of retreat where one prays through the *Spiritual Exercises* of St Ignatius. Part way through the retreat there is an exercise (the Kingdom Exercise) where one is invited to decide whether one chooses to follow Christ in the work of the Kingdom. At the end of it there is a prayer of offering – a prayer which I rewrote as,

> Yes, my Lord,
> Yes,
> it is my deliberate choice
> to let go of my burden
> to stop hiding
> to be me
> and to be at your service
> for your praise and glory
> and all this only for the sake of love.
> Amen.

As a way of recording my retreat I decided to do some tapestry. With my 'Yes' came a great sense of God's love and I wanted to pour myself back on him, to do an act of love. I felt like the woman in Luke 7 – wetting his feet with her tears and pouring ointment on him. I wanted to represent that love in a communion wafer – a host – and so the white host was stitched. It took four days . . . simply pouring love for Jesus into every stitch and as I dwelt on my love and desire for him God took me to the cross.

That afternoon I found myself being led to walk up the mountain behind the retreat house for the first time. As I walked through a gate there before me lay the sea and the mountains. I felt like Moses looking over the Promised Land. God was giving me his creation and there was a reminder for me – that love to be true is mutual, given and received. It was not enough for me to pour out love on him. I had also to receive his love.

What is fascinating, as I look back on that retreat and that episode, is not so much the desire to say yes, nor the recognition of the mutuality of love which is necessary for a healthy spiritual life but the fact that out of everything I could have chosen, I chose a host . . . that for me the host clearly represents, in a way nothing else can do, the full meaning, 'the height, depth, length and breadth', of the love of God.

The next of the exercises begins the training in discipleship by revealing more intensely Christ's own response of obedience to the Father. We are invited to pray with the birth narrative and to pray through the hidden life of Christ and then later through his ministry up to Palm Sunday. During this time a choice about one's life may also be made. During this part of the exercises we are asking to be captivated by the heart of Christ . . . and the exercises encourage us to discover the patterns of light and darkness in our lives – all the time seeking to discern the movement of God's spirit, in order to be drawn closer to the way of Christ.

Having said my 'Yes' I had then to pray with the visit of the angel to Mary and the birth of Christ. For me, the day was about immense and mutual love, echoing my experience on the mountain. When I thanked God for a very special day I sensed him say, 'Just remember – every time you say that you love me, remember that I loved you first.'

It was about this time in the retreat that I felt again a sense of calling and a sense of testing. I asked Jesus why I was being tested. The answer seemed to be, 'You are being tested to see if your calling is strong.'

I asked what kind of calling this might be, and the answer was simple: 'A life of prayer.'

It was too simple for me. I thought I'd got it wrong and for a while I struggled but gradually God showed me that all he wanted was my love . . . and he showed me how I hold him: in the baby of Bethlehem, in bread and wine, and in the crucified.

Together God and I reviewed the previous year – how I have struggled to resist the call to a life of prayer and how that struggle has at times seemed fierce and yet how all the time I have wanted to say 'Yes' to God.

And God reminded me that I had said 'Yes'.

In this retreat too – this retreat which has changed my life more clearly into a life of prayer – the Eucharist was again prominent, even central. To return to that poem by Veronica Zundel, my own experience has been that the Eucharist has drawn me out of hiding to stand open before God. It has called me to an ever-deepening relationship and filled me with delight. It has opened me to the treasures I had all along, whilst adding myriad meanings and intense love.

Having said all that, I return to the reality that sometimes it has no feeling at all. It is simply something God does and which I attend, but that is enough too.

Chapter 10

STUDY AND SCRIPTURE

IT'S AMAZING HOW SOME WORDS OF Scripture become truly ours –
they speak to us again and again through life. So I find myself going
back to words which first struck me when I was a teenager.

> In returning and rest you shall be saved;
> in quietness and in trust shall be your strength.
> (Isaiah 30:15)

These words have been used again and again to touch me at a deep
level and to change the course of my life. They have been alive and
active, 'sharper than any two-edged sword, piercing until it divides
soul from spirit, joints from marrow' (Hebrews 4:12). They
represent, for me, the power of Scripture in my life.

So what is this power and how do we engage with it? I suspect it
is when we let the Bible be *above* us – holding us – that we learn the
things of God, much in keeping with Jesus saying in John 6:45,
'They shall all be taught by God.' If we are to let Scripture shape us,
and form in us greater conformity and maturity in Christ, we need
to let the Word pierce us and so transform us. If this is the case we
need to let Scripture touch us on a daily basis. Indeed, we need to
go further, for I sense that Scripture is most likely to be a source of
grace to all people when we enter dialogue with it. Above all, I heed
Jesus saying, in John 5:39f, that we miss the point if we search the
Scriptures to find life only to miss that life-giving encounter with
him. Scripture has led me to know more of Jesus.

Scripture above us

Returning to Luke 24 and the two disciples on the road to Emmaus,
it always seems highly significant that Jesus broke the Scriptures

before he broke the bread. There is always the possibility of fresh revelation when we open God's Word and let it touch us not just in the intellect, though surely there, but also in the heart.

The image of the napkin from Chapter 1 highlights the fact that there are different ways of picking up a Bible. For my own part I choose not to pick up Scripture with the intention of finding specific texts to back or promote an argument. Rather, I pick it up gently, like a napkin, and let it unfold that I might see Jesus (John 12:21). Whatever I am reading I hope to find an encounter with the living God. As was said in Chapter 2: as we might gently open a napkin 'so we are to read Scripture. Our attention is to be on the face of God, listening with our soul to him. We are listening for the gentle voice, the voice of love.' In this there is a massive vulnerability to God, an attentiveness to his working in our lives. To return to Ignatius and his *Spiritual Exercises*, it is a recognition that we are not to claim riches, pride and honour[1] but rather find an attitude of gentle response to a gentle and tender God who invites us to spiritual (maybe actual) poverty, a share in his insults and injuries and humility. It suggests that Scripture, however much intellectual knowledge we may gain about it, only serves us when it makes us truly receptive to God and truly loving in response – loving of God and also loving in our lives – in true obedience to the Word.

In this, too, we are to follow Jesus, who was himself obedient to the Father's Word. It has been said of him that he is 'pure receptivity of the Father'.[2] Mary, too, knew what it was to know this contemplative attitude to God's Word. She knew the vulnerability, the piercing and the joy.

It was reflecting on her role, and the whole image of the baby being presented in the Temple, that led to a meditation on that scene found in the reading for Candlemass – Luke 2:22-35. In this meeting of Simeon and Mary, both are vulnerable to God's Word.

> Open my heart,
> Lord.
> Still my desires.
> Bring me to silence
> a deep pool of love.
> Let me plumb the depths
> of my being
> and there find your touch.

Let me lay against your breast
and in the silence of my heart
hear yours,
the beat, the eternal beat, of love.
Let me be vulnerable to your word.
Everything I think or feel or say,
shaped by your silence.
Let me find within
an abyss of love –
your love –
and diving down
enable me to extract the pearl of love
that others need.
By prayer, by love, by life, may I
reveal its presence
in the world's midst.
Not me, but you,
a steady heartbeat,
in a noisy world.
Carve out in me
a space, dear Lord,
a space 'Capax Dei'
that you may fill
to send my life-blood flowing
for your glory.
Let it be, Lord, let it be.

Allowing Scripture to pierce us

Reading Scripture is more than a literary or academic exercise. It has the possibility and potential of dynamic change in our life – 'Let me be vulnerable to your Word.' It may bring us pain or pleasure, joy or tears but it will, should we be vulnerable to its grace, enlighten us and draw us into the closer presence of God.

There's a lovely passage in Kenneth Leech's book, *Spirituality and Pastoral Care*, where he quotes Charles Marson writing about the dangers of knowing Scripture without entering this vulnerability. He writes about those '. . . who know all about Abraham except the way to his bosom, all about David except his sure mercies, and all about St Paul except the faith which he preached'.[3]

It's as though sometimes we fail to see the Word for the words. How easy it is to make Scripture a purely academic pursuit and then theology loses its essence, for true theology springs from the application not just of our intellect but of our whole selves. It is as much about praying as thinking and as much about living as either of the others – we are to be doers of the word and not just hearers.

To really study Scripture in this way is to understand that we can love with our minds and seek understanding with our hearts. Indeed, we are not fully alive unless we apply both to our study and prayer – both mind and heart need to be engaged, absorbed, in being contemplatively open to the loving Word of a loving God. I have often found that when I am at my most contemplative – silent, still, waiting on God – I need to study more rather than less, to keep a balance.

This allowing Scripture to pierce us means being quite relaxed as we listen to its cadences and imagine its images. Then God can speak not only through the words but through the spaces that lie between them.

In Chapter 2 we explored *Lectio Divina*. That is one way of allowing that to happen. Another, as we saw in Chapter 4, is simply to imagine the scene that the Bible depicts, e.g. one of the gospel stories, become a part of the scene and then, in imagination, speak with the characters.

It can be an amazing experience to find oneself holding in imagination the baby or the crucified Christ, to find oneself on the mountain of the Beatitudes and hear for oneself what Jesus is saying specifically to the poverty of our lives, or to sit at the Last Supper watching the faces of the disciples or having one's feet washed by this Lord of ours.

Allowing Scripture to touch us on a daily basis

All this suggests a personal involvement with Scripture. Somehow we need to let God look at us with love through his Scripture, and somehow we need to return that gaze. I think it was George Aschenbrenner who said that 'we become what we contemplate'. Preaching once, I based a sermon on that one comment. For one person, at least, it made an enormous impact. They reflected on what they contemplated on a daily basis – a particular newspaper, the TV and so on. Then they reflected on how much they contemplated

God. What helped them to change the balance of their gaze, and has helped me over many years, was the practice of reading Scripture each day in a prayerful context.

In recent years there have been explorations of how this might be done and many versions of the daily office and Bible notes are available. However, the central theme is the same – somehow we want to immerse ourselves in Scripture and let it resonate with the circumstances of our lives and of the world in which we are involved. That resonance may be slow and not mind-dazzlingly clear but over a period of years it can have a lasting and deep impact.

My own enjoyment of the daily office is simply that it encourages me to read portions of Scripture that have been chosen by somebody else and it takes me into corners of the Bible that I would not necessarily visit. In so doing, it keeps me open to the breadth and diversity of Scripture rather than returning only to the familiar and well-loved passages.

Such a vulnerability to Scripture raises issues which might otherwise be avoided and often leads either to further personal prayer or to study, in order to try to understand the background of particular passages and situations.

Indeed, intellectual study plays an important part too. It seems to me that we never solve Scripture – never find the indisputable truth of it – but are always open to the mystery of it. Our study, at whatever level, opens our eyes to fresh and illuminating truths as God seeks to shape and mould us, 'transformed by the renewing of our minds' (Romans 12:2). But acquisitive spirituality is a false lover when it draws us to intellectual knowledge or felt experience of God for its own sake. All is for the purposes of the Kingdom. We need only pray for that central grace of the *Spiritual Exercises* – 'an interior knowledge of our Lord, who became human for me, that I may love him more intensely and follow him more closely'.[4]

Entering dialogue

Interior knowledge of God implies a living relationship – and relationships imply communication and dialogue. So, in doing theology, dialogue is important. There is the dialogue within ourselves between intellectual knowledge, lived experience and prayerful insights. But there are two other layers of dialogue in using

Scripture in prayer – the ongoing dialogue with God and the dialogue with our fellow believers.

This dialogue within ourselves becomes a way of life. When we have studied and prayed with Scripture over a period it becomes part of the texture of our being. We find that whatever we are doing, words of Scripture emerge from within and encourage, challenge, console or attract us even in the middle of the busiest life. It is as though Scripture is part of the very texture of life for us – as our senses become aware of what is happening around us, so our spirit is engaging with the Word which is at work within us. The dialogue that emerges is life-giving, as we allow Scripture, life and prayer to mingle. It turns, necessarily, into colloquy – speaking with God as a person would with a friend.

I believe it is in this dialogue with Scripture that previously unnoticed facets of truth and fresh revelation evolve – revelations that speak to us in our day and circumstances. So often we seek to force Scripture into a straitjacket of meaning when, in fact, it is most life-giving when we allow it to speak freely to us, or rather allow God to speak freely through it.

So dialogue happens at many levels: the individual's encounter with Scripture in study and prayer; the wider encounter through liturgy and worship; the academic study; discussion and debate; and the dialogue with the tradition of scriptural interpretation. In all of this we are listening to each other and to the spirit who longs to reveal God's truth. Such dialogue demands humility in our approach both to Scripture and each other.

I was moved greatly in this understanding of prayer and Scripture by listening to a rabbi who spoke of how it *mattered to God* that we not only read Scripture but dialogue with it. It matters to God precisely because he wants opportunity to explore rather than impose truth, and he wants to explore *with us*. Here is a God consistent with Christ – a God who not only speaks the Word but makes himself vulnerable to us.

And now, as I write, I am reduced to silence. If I feel the texture of that silence I recognise it as the presence of Jesus. I am being reminded that all my words have a truth bursting to get out – the truth of the living Lord Jesus. It is he who wants to speak to us through the words, the silences, the living and the praying.

Finding Jesus

Scripture, and especially praying with Scripture, is so often the way that I, and those to whom I listen, find a new and living encounter with Jesus. In praying with the gospel accounts there is fresh opportunity to see Jesus for ourselves – no longer trying to relate only to religious hearsay.

For my own part this has been crucial. When my wife died in 1989 I felt that my relationship with God had been strengthened by the experience, and I still know that to be true. However, I was to find that, looking back, I had sidelined Jesus in my spiritual life. I had identified with the crucified, as many do in the midst of suffering, but I had lost the attractive Jesus. Though intellectually I still knew him to be loving, in my emotions I guess I was not so sure.

When I went on a retreat about eighteen months afterwards I found myself confronted through Scripture with his love. I reflected on where I had allowed his image to be distorted and was reminded of some of the well-meaning folk who had attempted to pressure Jackie and I into their own idea of what God wanted for us. There were the couple who almost chased Jackie around a hotel so that they could lay hands on her, and the minister who claimed to care deeply for her but apparently only as a means of exercising his healing ministry, not really as a person. Then, of course, there was the one who said that obviously Jackie was ill because either she or I had sinned.

Being a long-term carer has another, less obvious, because constant, spiritual undermining – the simple fact of continual exhaustion. So, on this retreat where I was physically cared for as well as given time to pray, God was able to speak afresh and he did it through daily prayer with Scripture.

Even as I write I am taken back to a particular prayer room and to the sense of his presence for me there. There I found myself – like a prodigal son – simply glad to be back and kneeling within the embrace which I had found difficult to feel, and hard to live without.

Scripture had taken me to a new encounter with the living Lord, an encounter which has inspired my life and ministry ever since; but once I had renewed my acquaintance with the loving Lord I found, of course, that he had been there all the time. Indeed, much of the identification with Jesus crucified, for those five years of being a carer, had prepared me for this more joyful encounter. Scripture does that. It digs deep and makes this space capable of containing God himself – 'Capax Dei'.

It invites us not just to become aware of the love he offers but to stay with that love and to live it as far as we are able:

> Let me not run from the love which you offer.
> Let me not run from the gifts that you offer.
> Let me not run from being willing to use
> the gifts I have been given in your service.
> Let me not run from knowing and showing your love.
> Let me follow my beautiful Christ.
> Let me follow him through risk and death
>   and revelation of self, if need be,
> for your sake and for your glory.
> Lord, give me courage,
>   Lord, give me faith,
>   Lord have mercy,
> Lord let me not hide,
>   except in you.

All that has been said here of Scripture as a means into prayer could also be said of much spiritual reading and study – we can allow God to use the words in order to pierce us with his love, to wound us with a desire for him.

In that wounding and desire our spiritual life finds its source and its destination.

Chapter 11

CONNECTEDNESS WITH HUMANITY

PRAYER IS ABOUT LIFE AND LIFE ABOUT PRAYER, so fundamental to my prayer is my sense of connectedness with humanity – with individuals, with the human condition and with what is happening on the broader scale.

Connectedness with individuals

When I was training at theological college I spent six weeks working as a nursing assistant in a hospice. Although we had seminars with eminent specialists, which have informed and invigorated my life and ministry, the real teachers were the patients. One in particular, Fred, still comes to mind although it is almost thirty years since I met him. Fred was the first person I met with Motor Neurone Disease. He needed complete care and could hardly speak.

One day I was asked to help bathe him. We got him carefully into the bath and he lay enjoying the warmth and support of the water. As he relaxed so he began to talk. It was often at such times that we talked about his death and the effect on his family, or maybe simply about our shared love of music. Nothing was out of bounds in our conversations – indeed that was the basis of the pastoral care we offered. We were there for the patients.

But that day Fred was there for me. Clearly he was a man of great intuition and insight for, though I had said nothing, he picked up that day that I was troubled. He made a comment, which reflected a very accurate perception, and then spoke some words of support. Nothing more was said and we carried on as before but it made me realise then that we cannot offer love unless we are prepared to be loved. We cannot serve others with authenticity and integrity unless we are willing to be served.

Recently, whilst reading Richard Cleaver's *Know My Name* I came across a paragraph that took me back those many years, back to the bath and Fred:

> Vincent de Paul told us to do the works of mercy in such a way that the poor can forgive us for the bread we give them. This is why Jesus went to eat with sinners. He offered his loving company and accepted their love in return. Unless we are willing to receive it in return, love is turned into something else we inflict on others.[1]

Prayer is about mutual love and so shows itself in practice in mutual love. Although we are often in situations where the balance is on one person offering to be there for another in a professional relationship there still needs to be the ability to receive as well as give, lest we 'inflict' condescension and pity, rather than love and respect.

There is a mutuality of love in other relationships too.

As a curate I visited a school for disabled children. I was surrounded by love there, though I knew, from visiting parents, that this love was costly. One of the girls who had never spoken in her life became ill and died. I was asked, as a priest who knew her and the family, to take the funeral. As I gazed around the packed church I realised what an impact this girl had made on so many people. Somehow she had given all of us a most precious gift. For each of us the gift was special and unique but I wanted to try to see if there was a common gift too. Looking at the faces before me I could see only love. I began my address with the simple words, 'Sarah evoked love.' The church went silent and people began to nod. I did not need to say much more. Sarah had evoked love at a deep level in many people. People had found resources in themselves that they did not know they possessed. Her gift of grace to them was to release those resources. I still reflect on Sarah and her life in my prayer. Here is someone who taught me more than I can say, simply by being a part of my life. Yes, I was the ordained minister but she ministered to me too.

As I reflect on her again I realise how she connected me with another level of our humanity, and as always prayer followed life and I was able to pray at that level. There are no words there – simply a holding of persons before God, in gratitude and love.

The other image that comes to mind as I reflect on people who have taught me about God and prayer is the image of rainbow-coloured wellington boots. They are, for me, a symbol of how God reaches out to us at times of need. Let me explain. When Jackie became ill we had already had lots of illness in the family and both her parents had died. Apart from her sister, Jackie only had a few elderly aunts. One of them, Aunt Edna, stepped in to help. She would visit on a monthly basis, staying for a weekend. Those visits became a lifeline. She brought not just herself and her wisdom, which was immense, she brought humour and fun. Though she had never had children herself she quickly established herself as the children's friend, so when she wanted to take them down to the beach she decided that she needed wellington boots. We imagined her coming back from her shopping expedition with black ones or maybe green ones. Instead she came back with rainbow-coloured ones.

Somehow, through those years she came to life as a result of the care she offered us and we came to life watching her and enjoying life with her. When she died, a year before Jackie, after contracting cancer, we buried not just an aunt but a great friend, confidant and inspiration.

Here again was the gift of human grace – of prayer in action as we dared to dance the joyful dance of humanity in the face of disease and death.

Since then I have married again and been divorced. Though my ex-wife and I are still friends I have had to learn to accept that sense of failure and grief that a failed marriage brings. I have found this too makes connections with others. Perhaps between estranged couples there is more need for human grace than is sometimes acknowledged. If we are to provide security for the children there is no room for self-serving antagonism.

Above all, this kind of connectedness with humanity makes us realise the need of God's grace and forgiveness – not in a grovelling way but in the way of realism. We simply cannot move on without the gift of grace – so in prayer we hold the sense of failure and need of each of the people involved.

Having been widowed and divorced before the age of fifty means that I have been able to offer my experiences back to God in prayer and invite him to use them in my ministry – not necessarily in a direct way but in the sense of allowing a sense of empathy and a listening ear that is sharpened by experience. And there is no room for any sense of superiority – I have known failure as well as much joy. Life has shaped me and God, I pray, uses the 'me' so moulded.

And life, of course, moves on. There is, in being single, always the possibility of meeting a new partner and certainly the opportunities to make new friends.

The grace of friendship is a necessary one if we are to grow in love. On moving to a new area of the country I found myself separated from my usual circle, so, when, after a fairly barren time, I made a new friend I found myself again set free:

> So suddenly,
> I am free to love
> at depth
> again.
>
> Where had it gone
> not the sense of being loved
> but of my loving . . . ?
> I wanted to
> I tried
> I did
> in action
> but feeling?
> No.
>
> It's come back
> with so much
> JOY
> and laughter
> is in the air.
> Why?
> Why, dear God,
> because you gave me
> love in flesh . . .
> someone who has shown,
> does show me love.
> And I am whole again
> and glad to be alive.

Love has taken me captive
and set me free
bound me to another
and opened me to all.

In close friendship, in that kind of friendship where we can be
totally open and free in our conversation, where we need wear no
masks, I believe we are set free to assume our full humanity but
also to connect with all other people. One friendship at depth binds
us to one other person but, as the poem says, opens us to all.

What it also does is open us up to God again, for in finding love
enfleshed for us we are brought to gratitude and understanding,
love and self-offering.

Connectedness with the human condition

We are linked with others in sorrow and joy, but we are linked at an
even more fundamental level – linked solely on the basis of our
humanity. As Carl Rogers pointed out, what is most personal is
most likely to be most universal.

I believe that, when we pray, when we hold our deepest joys,
fears and fantasies before God, we can do so on behalf of all people.
More essential is that when we actually choose to follow Christ,
when we choose to align ourselves with the Kingdom, we commit
ourselves to that interior struggle between that which is of God and
that which is not of God.

That struggle can be intense if we dare to enter any extended
silence. Once all the normal distractions and illusions are banished,
when busyness is no longer used to avoid facing what lies in our
heart, then we find ourselves caught between the drives of our lives
and the attraction of Christ.

It is here, in the struggle, that the need for discernment is greatest and we realise how important it is to listen to the voice of love,
to that calmer inner voice which calls us to life among the storms
that may be raging within and without.

This listening prayer has been a growing part of my prayer. What
am I listening to? I suspect I am listening to the voice of God,
though I hear no voice. What I hear is a mixture of voices – voices
of people who love me, voices of those who challenge me, my own
inner voice, and the voice of Scripture and church. Among these

voices I listen for those intimations of God that I discern to be consistent with the God whom I have come to know through my life of
prayer and whom I recognise in those to whom I listen.

This is another aspect of being connected with humanity and the
human condition – the God I know is not just my God made in my
own image but is the God that others encounter too. It is for this
reason that I believe the spiritual journey needs to be undertaken
always in the company of others, though simultaneously undertaken for oneself alone. It is in the interrelationship between our
own experience and that of others that our discernment is honed
and focused.

What is happening on the broader scale

When I was confirmed at the age of fifteen I was given a confirma-
tion book, which suggested various ways of praying – the traditional
ACTS (Adoration, Confession, Thanksgiving and Supplication). I
found it, even then, to be a way of prayer that did not help me.
Prayer was already something I did naturally and trying to impose
a structure of this kind deadened the prayer rather than brought it to
life.

Supplication, praying for ourselves and others, seemed to me to
be something one did quite naturally in a way which suited the rest
of our prayer. As someone who has used many kinds of prayer, but
who reverts to silence more often than not, intercession can feel
threatening if it is felt to be about making specific requests of God.
However, this connectedness with humanity suggests that there
may be another way of interceding – simply holding situations
and people before God and linking our internal struggle with the
universal struggle to see all that is godly emerge out of the world's
confusion and pain.

This 'holding of people and situations' can be a costly form of
intercession for it does not presume to know what is best for others
but simply trusts that, held in God, whatever happens can be used
for good.

My own experience is that this sometimes involves being prepared to hold some of the 'darkness' so that others may be freed to
move forward. So this is not a passive kind of prayer. It very much
involves us not only in the prayer but in the process of conflict

between the various spirits. In praying we become part of the answer to prayer.

When I have been praying for a person I have often found myself experiencing movements in my own spirit that do not relate to my own life circumstances. If I am alert I sometimes become aware of that and consider people for whom I am praying. I often find that my spirit has been intuiting their journey and responding to it. I am conscious too that others who have accompanied me have carried some of my difficult times in this way.

One particular friend who has accompanied me through much, first as a spiritual director and then as a friend, has often phoned at moments when she could not possibly know what was happening but because she has recognised this process operating in her spirit. These have often been moments of pure grace when I have been brought to see how wonderfully God uses us to offer support and strength to each other. It is a level of intercession that often staggers me.

World events can also play a part in our prayer in this way. We may simply offer them to God, not casually but with the intention of letting our spirit be used. Whilst armies fight battles, people of intercession are operating at a very different level in the hope of seeing good triumph. That isn't to say they always see what they desire, but rather that they trust in the ultimate triumph of good over evil and long, with all their being, to play their part in friendship with Christ.

It is in this area that I value highly the lives of those people who give themselves totally to prayer. I have in mind those religious who live the enclosed life and there, on behalf of us all, enter this interplay of light and shadow, and hold out, trusting only in the love of a God who loves us infinitely.

In my own life the Sisters of the Love of God, based at Fairacres in Oxford, were those who first revealed to me the importance and immense value of this ministry. Over several years I visited them regularly and they were a great support when Jackie died, not only by their prayer, though knowing that they were praying was often what saw me through the night, but also by their fun.

After Jackie died I took the children down to meet the community. We had an amazing weekend of sheer love and immense humour. It reminds me that much of my own connectedness with humanity is revealed not only in the depth and seriousness of the conflict within, but is found also in sheer outrageous laughter.

When I was a student at theological college I annoyed one particular tutor immensely by quoting again and again in my essays a comment by the playwright Dennis Potter.

> I am drawn towards God by something that is very light-hearted and something that is very anguished and I think that a collision between the two things inside of myself will reveal to me not just what I believe but what I actually am.

This comment on a TV chat show continues to resonate in me and feed me. I believe that in God, in prayer and in life we make connections by humour and fun as well as by the quieter and deeper things of life. But more, I believe that if we are to dare to enter depth and silence we need laughter as a balance. A good belly laugh gives perspective like nothing else!

Not surprisingly then, I love the quotation from Meister Eckhart, who answers our query about what goes on in the heart of the most Holy Trinity:

> In the core of the Trinity the Father laughs –
> and gives birth to the Son;
> The Son laughs back at the Father –
> and gives birth to the Spirit;
> The whole Trinity laughs –
> and gives birth to us[2]

and I happily consider myself a fool for Christ – happy to live with life's paradox – the conundrum of contraries:

> Let us be fools for Christ's sake.
> In facing the truth,
> May we be set free from illusion;
> In accepting our wounds
> May we make others whole;
> In embracing the outcast,
> May we be known ourselves, redeemed;
> In discovering our child,

May we grow to full stature;
In seeking true innocence,
May we no longer harm;
In yielding to dying,
May we know love's pain and joy;
In the folly of the cross,
May we see the wisdom of God.[3]

Chapter 12

MYSELF

LOOKING BACK ON LIFE IT'S EASY TO SEE THAT, however much I like people, I am a natural loner. Thinking of books I have read, I realise that years and years ago I was struck by Howard Spring's *All the Day Long*, where a character says something like, 'Do what we are alone we are lone and the sooner we learn to live with that, the sooner we are capable of living with others.' Then, looking at my book of quotes, I find another one from Thomas Mann:

> A solitary, unused to speaking of what he sees and feels, has mental experiences which are at once more intense and less articulate than those of a gregarious man. They are sluggish, yet more wayward, and never without a melancholy tinge. Sights and impressions which others brush aside with a glance, a light comment, a smile, occupy him more than their due; they sink silently in, they take on meaning, they become experience, emotion, adventure. Solitude gives birth to the original in us, to beauty unfamiliar and perilous – to poetry, but it also gives birth to the opposite; to the perverse, the illicit, the absurd.[1]

Somehow, through this interesting, sometimes fearful territory of myself, God prays. It *is* God who prays. Of that I am sure. It is as if I have no choice but to pray. It is as natural as breathing. No wonder then that the Lenten hymn 'Christian, dost thou see them?' with its line, 'while I breathe, I pray' strikes such a deep chord (and provides the inspiration for the book title).

God prays through anything and everything, as we have seen. He uses all of life to reveal himself and evoke a response of wonder, love, discipleship and awe. So often, when I have tried to distract myself by reading a novel or watching a film, God has come through a word underlined or an image highlighted.

The film *Shadowlands* – that beautiful account of the relationship between C. S. Lewis and Joy Davidson – provides the perfect example. It is a film I have much valued and admired. On watching it for the third or fourth time it spoke profoundly about this whole area of prayer. C. S. Lewis is challenged by his colleagues about prayer and simply responds,

> I pray because I can't help myself.
> I pray because I'm helpless.
> I pray because the need flows out of me all the time,
>   waking and sleeping.
> It doesn't change God, it changes me.

This then is my belief about myself and prayer – I can't help myself because God prays in me, though he needs me to be receptive. It is that receptivity which evokes my prayer. I can't help but pray because I am helpless, receptive to his touch. He uses all of life to help me pray but all my prayer, even for a lifetime, will not change God at all, though he cares passionately about it. It will change me.

God prays in us

Jesus told the disciples of the need to pray always and never to lose heart (Luke 18:1). He had told them before of the need to pray: to knock, to ask, to seek, never to give up, to trust that the heavenly Father will listen to his children and give them the Holy Spirit. But to pray always? How can we begin? As I type the words I feel my fingers merely grazing the keys on the keyboard – a reminder of the risk and the vulnerability of talking about prayer, of putting words around that which is so often without words and which is unique to each one of us. How can we pray without ceasing? We need perhaps to ask a different question: 'If Jesus is praying in us unceasingly, how can we become aware?' Light dawns; the emphasis has moved. Him not us. His prayer, not ours. I am nothing, *Nade*. He is everything, *Todo*. 'The abyss of our nothingness cries aloud to the abyss of God's infinity, and they meet in a kiss.'[2] Wherever we are, whatever life is throwing at us or against us, whatever the darkness or the light that we experience, he is praying.

Calm and still be.
Deep silence.
Hush
Listen.
Let all distractions cease.
Listen carefully. Hush
Let heart's ear open be.
Body be still,
Mind's busyness pause.
Listen to a soul
Quiet at her prayer.

God needs us to be receptive

Bishop Theophan the Recluse writes, 'the principal thing is to stand before God with the mind in the heart and to go on standing before him.'[3] To stand before him. This is prayer – to stand with the angels in the presence of God and go with the angels with love for others. To go out from standing still, to pray and to love, to pray and to live, is to see life as a whole – not one and then the other but of a piece, whole and holy. To stand before God is to listen to the heart's prayer, to discover the river of prayer that is already flowing and into which we may go, but which we cannot claim as our own. The flow of the river of prayer is the work of the spirit, praying in groans too deep for words, the prayer of Jesus interceding at the right hand of the Father, the movement of love at the heart of the Trinity, the movement of love overflowing in us. Prayer is nothing but love, nothing but standing in the river of prayer and love which is the Godhead, and holding our mind in our heart. It is a beautiful image of integrity – to hold our mind still but to let all our thoughts and imaginings be held in the deepest centre of our being where we may experience the very heart of the Trinity.

However we pray, whatever posture we adopt, whatever patterns of prayer we have found helpful, it is to this deep encounter within with the living God that our life aspires. To reach a state of unceasing prayer may take a lifetime. It will be enough for now if we acknowledge our willingness to let him love us into prayer, if we acknowledge our desire to pray unceasingly, if we dare to love each other and the world for his sake, if we give time to praying whatever way we can, and if we give time even when we can't pray.

It will be enough for now. As we have seen, it will take us with Christ into the realm of conflict between that which draws us to God and that which does not, both within us and without. It will draw us to a deep place of encounter within, which will sustain us through the dry times, allowing us to trust in his praying when we feel we cannot pray. It will enable us to trust in his faithfulness when our faith seems as elusive as the morning mist. A Carmelite nun writes,

> In coming to prayer you must put yourself in the presence not of something but of someone; you have confrontation not with an idea; you are face to face with a living being who listens to you, speaks to you and prepares to give you everything. In fact you stand before the face of the living God.[4]

Receptivity evokes prayer

People are sometimes surprised, because I am an Anglican, by my devotion to Mary. Mary for me is not the sentimental Mary of some of the images, not the over-pious Mary of some of the statues. She is simply the one who reveals what it means to be truly receptive to God – one could be no more receptive than to bear the child which is the fruit of union with another. She is receptive, not passive. She plays a full part in the birth of Jesus. She will bring him to birth, nurture, cherish and teach this child and she will hold him in her arms when he is taken from the cross and meet him when he is risen.

To be receptive, then, is not to be a victim but to be vulnerable to God and his Word – vulnerable because one *chooses* to be so. The choice is important, as it always is. To choose is to assert one's full humanity and to choose to be vulnerable to God is the way in which we assert our divine humanity – that we are the beloved daughters and sons of the living and loving God.

This, then, can be our choice in life – to choose to follow a heartfelt, body-sensed, mind-embraced desire for God. It is a choice I have discovered I have to make again and again in all sorts of situations and it always inspires my prayer – leading me into a deeper truth of my being but also to the hermitage within – that still place within where I encounter God:

I have walked into my truth
my deepest calling . . .

This deepest truth
guides me in God's way,
leads me into love
yet cannot be conveyed . . .

And following its lead I know myself
walking into life
and in the hermitage within
a freedom of love and joy springs
even in the darkness.

God uses all of life to help us pray

This 'hermitage of the heart' is a very hidden place, which is left only for God and the self. Though hidden, it produces a depth of love that changes the way we approach life – a love that is often felt by others even when we feel nothing ourselves. It is also a prayerful centre that is maintained despite the traumas and storms of life. Because it is there, God can use everything that life throws against us to reveal himself.

Reflecting on what I have written I realise, as always, that much of my growth in prayer happened during Jackie's illness and in the period afterwards when I looked back over it and entered conversation with God about it. I suspect this is true for most of us – there are a few key events in life that really shape our prayer and attitude to God, and our understanding of him.

I have so often entered life with God by the wounds of my life, as well as by the joys. Entering by the wounds is less acceptable to many and yet, so often, as I listen to people in spiritual direction, I realise that it is the experience that many people have. In the Middle Ages there was a great devotion to the wounds of Christ and a recognition that it was often by the wounds that we come to know God. It was in reading about that period that I found myself writing:

We enter by the wounds of Christ.
He invites us to enter his wounded side,

Majestically,
As royal sons and daughters
entering his side with full honours
as a Princess may enter the Palace,
as a Prince walks
through the realm.

We enter by his wounds,
the broken hands
holding our broken hands
and drawing us in . . .

Wounds such as these are places where love and pain intermingle for,
as we shall discuss later, love and pain are not exclusive. Our wounding is often the place of meeting of these two great mysteries – mysteries we shall, in this life, never fathom, and yet will experience. So,
our wounding is not the place for careless words, for it is often that
which is most personal in us. Indeed, our wounding may be life-long
and normally kept hidden from others – often it is like Paul's thorn
in the flesh. At other times the wounding is more obvious.

If we know our own wounding then we may come before the
wounds of Christ.

We enter by his wounds.
He stumbles as he greets us,
his feet torn with nails.
He needs us to let him
lean on us,
when really it is we
who lean on him.

We enter by his wounds
bearing our darkness
into the blackness of
Good Friday
to find that the wounds,
his and ours,
have been the entrance,
ugly or beautiful?
to heaven.

And if wounding is the entrance to heaven? What do I mean? Simply, from my own experience, that wounding has the potential of being the place where we may most truly encounter God, because wounding is the place where pretence fails us. If we dare to encounter God in this place and seek his compassion, then, in the silence of shared mystery and love and the honesty of expressed pain and anger, we may grow.

This place of meeting is also the place where we can offer everything to God. On a desert retreat, one where all aids to prayer are removed and one is left with silence, I found myself gazing at Jesus on the cross:

> I gaze on him
> with longing.
> He hangs there
> dead and yet alive.
> Vibrant
> – his pain and love
> transfigured
> full humanity revealing divinity.
>
> This is what I seek
> so to enter my humanity
> to embrace all my frailty
> that there
> at the centre
> I may find myself at one with God.
>
> I gaze on him,
> I allow him to
> take away everything
> even my desire
> and still I find
> my being yearns for him,
> cries 'Yes' to him
> even from the darkness
> and this, I know, is gift.

This is what I seek: 'so to enter my humanity, to embrace all my frailty, that there at the centre I may find myself at one with God' –

these are words of seeking to live positively with wounding – with the thorn in the flesh. The words still pierce me some six years after that retreat. This was my desire then and remains my desire – to enter my full humanity and embrace all my frailty, that God may use the whole of life to pray in me. And this desire actually provokes me into prayer. It will not leave me alone but prompts me into prayer in all situations and at all times – God's doing, not mine.

Prayer will change us

All our prayer for a lifetime will not change God at all, though he cares passionately about it. It will change us. The difficulty about all this is trying to write about what is beyond words and trying to give a true account whilst realising that the depth and reality of what God does in our lives is often only seen, if at all, after the events have happened. For instance, in looking after Jackie there were obviously days when I simply did not know how to keep going. Looking after four children under seven would be enough, without caring for a person who was becoming increasingly disabled. So there is no triumphalism here. God did not take away the pain and distress but he was with us through it – Emmanuel – and he used it to draw us all, including Jackie, closer to himself.

So my prayer did not change anything. It changed everything. It did not change the long days and nights of slog. It did not change the constant questioning and fear about what would happen next. It did not change the procedures that had to be endured, nor the frustrations of dealing with bureaucracy.

But it changed everything. Jackie's outlook still amazes me – summed up nowhere better than in her poem about death:

> Today
> I face
> death.
>
> This disease, once creeping silently,
> now gallops callously.
> I am seen to stumble
> and we are all embarrassingly aware.

But today
I also have
a choice.

Life is now like being on
a children's slide at the park.
There is only one direction to go in.
I am falling,
and I can't get off.
I am sliding into eternity.

But I can let go of the sides
and lift my face
To feel the sun's caress,
the wind in my hair.
And, as I go,
scatter the fresh spring flowers
from my lap
to those who care to
stop
and watch
and
enjoy the fun.[5]

For me too, everything was changed. The experience has marked
me and changed all of those who were closely involved in caring for
Jackie and the family. Somehow prayer, uttered often through
clenched teeth or begun in good faith but ending in sleep, had
played its part – prayer which did not, at the time, bear any apparent fruit but which, with hindsight, kept the door open for God's
gaze of love and our response.

Chapter 13

TEARS

IT'S HARD TO DRIVE YOUR CAR WHEN tears are streaming down
your face. I remember the day still. Jackie, my wife, was having
innumerable tests to see what was causing her increasing paralysis.
After eighteen months we got a diagnosis – Motor Neurone
Disease. By then all emotion had been spent it seemed and we
accepted it calmly – glad, at last, to put a name to this invader of our
lives.

It was a day or two later that I was driving along a familiar route
and it hit me, making the tears come. This is one kind of tears – the
tears of emotion, of loss, of grief. But I have come to know another
kind of tears – a prayerful experience of feeling close to truth – close
to the truth of God and close to the truth of another person. In both
cases I find tears coming to my eyes. For years I kept quiet about
it, thinking that maybe it was just another sign of my being weak.
But then I discovered that it was not an uncommon experience and
that indeed in the Christian tradition these tears are recognised as
gift.

Tears of encounter

It is said of St Ignatius that he would be lost in devotion to the
Trinity, especially at the Eucharist,

> Entering the chapel and overwhelmed with a great devo-
> tion to the Most Holy Trinity, with very increased love and
> intense tears, without seeing the Persons distinctly as in
> the last two days, but perceiving in one luminous clarity a
> single Essence I was drawn entirely to its love, and later,
> while preparing the altar and vesting, great devotion and

tears, grace always assisting with much satisfaction of
soul.[1]

These prayerful tears of encounter do satisfy the soul. They cleanse
the soul – as though all our longing and all our sorrow for the past
converge and find a place of acceptance and healing. They wash out
our soul, leaving greater space for God. As the Jewish proverb says,
'What soap is for the body, tears are for the soul.' They are pure gift
and come only by God's grace and never at our bidding. Knowing
that they are often misunderstood by others,[2] I have found myself
fighting them as I lead worship – with greater or lesser success.

> Is there a choice?
> Can I not love?
> Can I not gaze upon his face
> and fall again in love?
> Can I *choose* to let tears flow,
>   to make them stop
> when, gazing on his face, his eyes
> I find myself absorbed in love?
> Can I walk away?
> It would be to choose to die.
> O Yes, there are times
> when for love of Him
> I hold myself from gazing
> in order to serve His way
> – contain myself
> that others may be free.
> But to choose to turn away
> rather than RISK
> rather than LIVE
> would be to die
> would be *the* sin.
> So let me gaze on Him
> and let Him choose.
> Let Him water love with tears,
>   or hold them back.
> Let me listen to His voice,
>   His will
> – to risk or to contain,

to overflow with love,
or take the quiet stance
        of waiting.
His will, not mine be done.
    His love,
        His joy,
            His peace
be what others see,
        not me.
Let me be as glass –
    transparent to His being
open and vulnerable to His love,
        complete surrender.

This is my desire,

    Nothing more.

        Nothing less.

This is my desire –

Christ, and him alone.

Nothing, nothing but Him.

These then, several years ago and recorded from my journal, are the tears of encounter, but sometimes in these tears there is also sorrow. Sr Margaret Magdalene illuminates this gift of tears when she writes, 'It is far more a convergence of a desperate yearning, a terrible long-ing for God, and a piercing sorrow for the sin that "wounds his love and mars his image in us".'[3]

As gift these tears may last an instant or an hour – or may go on, intermittently, for days and then not re-occur for years. They take us by surprise – arising often at times when life has undergone change and seems more in line with the perceived will of God:

        For a while today,
        my whole being has been pain
        and tears unnumbered
        no bottle could contain.

And why?
Now that I feel at home,
now that God is so close
our love so deep,
so clear.

I lay upon my bed and
held myself,
wordless,
but full of love
before my God
and let the pain be felt.

And then I saw,
in all these
twenty years when I have not been
totally at home in him
when I have let myself be
held from him a distance
in order to serve him more
he has held the pain away from me
but now I am at home
the pain is felt and tears flow
for love and gladness, joy and peace.
Complete surrender
to his will.

And in the two deep sounding notes –
intimacy and distance,
love and pain
there is a perfect harmony,
and in the recognition, joy
and in the joy I see his face
and know his heart bears me
and always has.

So they are always tears of encounter – of meeting God deeply. They
come not only through prayer and worship, though often the
Eucharist is a place of tears, but through encounters with other
people. Sometimes that encounter is one which ministers directly to

us and sometimes it is at times when, supposedly, we are ministering
to others.

After a long period of wilderness in life, a time of barrenness in
relationships, somebody looked at me with love. It was only a
glance, fleeting and transitory, but highly significant:

> Tears are here again.
> Of love or pain?
> I cannot tell,
> only sense, deep down, the movement,
> feel the salt of ages
> touching raw the eyes
> and know a flood is near.
>
> What opened me to this
>   torrent of core-feeling?
> Love was the culprit,
> the face of love,
> the look of love in someone's eyes,
> acceptance of the me long hid from view.
> Love was the culprit,
> acceptance in those eyes
> reflected in my heart,
> urging new life into my limbs, into entire being
> – fire overcoming anguish.
> Tears are here again,
> feelings emerging from the numbness
> of the pain beyond pain.
> Long dead dry bones
> feeling the gentle stirring of life-giving breath,
> longing to reach the promised life
> the land of plenty after so much desert.
> Tears are here again,
> abandonment to love,
>   to Christ.
> the only place to be
> and trusting in abandonment
> the challenge and the joy.

Here, as ever, though the tears stem from an encounter with another
person, the tears bring me back to encounter with God – more than

encounter – to an abandonment and a desire to give back, to serve, to live God's life. I find the same is true when tears catch me by surprise as I encounter beauty, or when I am listening to others in spiritual direction.

Beauty and truth

When I reflect on the question, 'When else do tears come?', I realise that increasingly they come when I see somebody being truly them-selves – for instance, watching somebody give themselves fully to art or music. The beauty may not be directly in the art or music itself but the fact that the person has found a means of expressing what is most personal for them.

I am reminded, as I write, of a young woman who, having completed her degree in engineering, has now begun training at art college. There is something very fragile about the transition, yet there is beauty too – beauty in seeing how she is able to express her-self and communicate with others through her new venture.

My mind goes back to being chaplain of a music school.[4] The school encouraged gifted youngsters in playing string instruments. On a Sunday afternoon I would lead a short service and the young people would either play or sing. I have seldom known such an intense sense of beauty and tears would often come unbidden – silent tears of no great emotion but piercing and painful beauty.[5]

As I reflect on that experience I realise that the beauty was two-fold. There was first of all the beauty of the music itself, which was often exquisite and stayed in the memory in such a way as to still be strong twenty years later. The young people had been trained not only to sing but to have a feel for and understanding of the words. It would often take the breath away. But there was also this deeper beauty – the recognition that, as Gerard Manley Hopkins knew, 'Christ plays in ten thousand places, Lovely in limbs and lovely in eyes not his.'[6]

These youngsters were being encouraged to be fully themselves – able fully to express their own beauty through the discipline of music. I would stand transfixed, often unable to go on until I had composed myself again. Here was what it means to be human – to find and express the beauty of the soul which is Christ within.

Tears have come even as I write this, for this is an experience which, though transitory, has lasting effects and draws me closer to

God, leaving me full of gratitude, praise and a desire to give back –
to serve – a theme to which we will return.

What do these tears signify? Quite simply, a recognition of the
beauty of true humanity.

Only a few days ago I was watching TV and a young singer[7] was
talking about his craft. He was teaching others and telling them of
the need to give everything to their music. Although I had enjoyed
his music I had not, before, seen him as he sang. Here was a young
man opening his soul as he sang. It was in the words, in his face and
in his voice . . . and was immensely beautiful beyond the music
itself. Here was someone not afraid to be himself, but rejoicing in
the self that he was and in the gift that he had. There seemed to me
to be beauty and truth in the performance and I found myself
profoundly moved.

Listening to others

I find the same beauty and truth when listening to other people.
When people tell their story there may be a whole gamut of emotions expressed. I can listen to all of that without being moved to
tears. When, however, people experience a new truth in their lives,
in their self-understanding or in their knowledge of God – when
people articulate something of the beauty at the core of their
being – then I find the tears begin to flow.

I think of a lady who came to see me for the first time. She began
by telling me of her deep sense of being called by God to some kind
of ministry. She recounted how she had faced many obstacles and
had left behind her well-paid profession, her home and much else.
Then we began to talk about who was calling her . . . and why she
had done all of this. She spoke of her relationship with Jesus – being
crazy in love with him and yet here was an incredibly practical
person who recognised the vulnerability of her position and yet
could not do other than follow the one who called. As she spoke, the
realisation then dawned that the Jesus she described was the very
same Jesus I encounter time and again as I listen to others.

Silence, deep silence, as I listened then and as I write now – the
silence I know to be the only response to this truth-beauty which I
find as I encounter people who have themselves met and are
articulating this meeting with God.

I have recognised my tearful response – gentle, silent, steady tears which are often unnoticed by the other – to be a kind of prayer. It is my spirit responding to their spirit and to the indwelling spirit of God. Tears are my prayer, expressing gratitude, sheer humility at the greatness of the gift, a longing love and a desire to respond.

It is as if one is held, embraced and gazed at by God, and as though there are no words adequate to the task of responding. Instead of words one's whole spirit wells up and tears begin to flow.

Words are not enough to describe this experience. So, as often happens when I find words inadequate to describe what I am trying to convey, I turn to a more poetic form – a reflection not just of when I listen but when I have experienced another truly listen to me.

> Listen now,
> to the silence
> descending
> falling
> upon us.
> Listen
> beyond our listening
> to each other.
> Our God is listening
> and truth is emerging
> gently in the silence.
> Words,
> that before have only been threads
>   in someone's memories
>   of pain and fear
>   even joy
> are woven now
> into texture of truth
> and find acceptant love
>   the possibility of beauty
>   the taste of splendour.
> In this listening silence
>   personhood is affirmed
> and timid truth encouraged
> by gentle loving.
>
> Deep stillness.
> Eternity the feel.

No time, no space,
but full of presence.
Just here, now,
and from the deep well of heart
engaging heart
engaging God –
tears.

Tears.
Tears of wonder and delight.
Tears of longing
   for the release of that beauty
long ensnared by prison bars of fear
   and solid walls of pain.
My tears are prayer
that in our meeting
you may be you,
you, loved by God,
you, beautiful
you free.

There is something about these prayerful tears that I realise takes all of me, engages every part of me in the listening and in the endeavour to love beyond my ability to love – reaching beyond myself in the way that Scott Peck suggests. He speaks of true spiritual growth coming through the exercise of real love, with love defined as 'the will to extend oneself for the purpose of nurturing one's own or another's spiritual growth'.

They are the tears of grace – of God's loving beyond my loving – so that often I feel that rather than do anything I have been done unto. If I have loved the person to whom I listen, and that I assume is the basis of spiritual direction, then somehow in that loving I too have been loved.

And yet, though I affirm and recognise that this is God's gift and grace, I also know that to listen in this way and with these tears all of us is being used so that, later, there is a level of exhaustion which needs attention. Deep nurture is required in our own souls, maybe through silent prayer, music, nature, art or someone who shows love to us.

This prayer of tears reminds me more than most of the corporate nature of ministry – of the need to be held by others, listened to by others, loved by others.

Eucharist

In the context of prayerful tears and being nurtured we are taken back to the Eucharist – to those moments when the gathered community takes together bread and wine and opens themselves up to the presence of Jesus.

> For a moment
> as I held the Host.
> It was not me
> but Him.
> Overwhelmed with love,
> I stood, silent, waiting,
> unable to move on.
> Lost, in love,
> in His presence.
> People waited in the silence.
> I could do nothing,
> but sensing the need
> I moved on.
> More words
> His, not mine . . .
> Body, Blood, *given* for you.
> Him, not me.
> Silence, not words.
> Love of the heart,
> not reason.
> Tears, loving tears,
> joyful spring of life
> poured out by Him through me.
> A confirmation of my 'Yes'
> to be alone,
>   all one,
>   for Him,
>   only for Him.

Tears of vulnerability

Writing this chapter reminds me of the vulnerability of writing about this area – an area I explored with Vanessa Herrick in a book we eventually called *Jesus Wept*[8] – a title which itself affirms that tears were part of Jesus' ministry too.

So why would one hesitate? Partly because this whole area is open to such misunderstanding. We are not talking here of simply being moved emotionally as one might be by a romantic film or an act of worship, where emotions are running high. This is not an experience that is at all manufactured. It simply happens. Nor is it an experience to be desired for its own sake. It only makes sense within an active following of Christ, a committed discipleship.

Like the other gifts of the spirit it can so easily become a badge of credibility (or incredibility depending on one's viewpoint). Ignatius was dealing with that when he wrote to Father Nicholas Goundanus, a man who longed for the gift of tears. He is told that the gift of tears is not necessary for the work of a disciple. All that is needed is a heart 'full of the desire of helping souls' and he says of those who have the gift of tears that, 'this does not mean that they have greater charity or that they are more effective than others who have no tears'.

For myself, there are many times when I wish tears did not come. It can be difficult to hide them and often leaves others bewildered. But if they are a gift you have been given then you assume God has a purpose in it. I write about them solely to encourage others who know this gift to see it as a gift of prayer – and a gift of being able to see great beauty and feel that beauty in its piercing intensity as a longing for God and as a desire to abandon oneself to his will and service.

This gift of tears seems to be primarily about a sense of being inflamed with love for God in himself or in his creation, with a consequent sense of compunction – that sense of sorrow for the time one has spent away from God. When there is an emotion it is that of piercing beauty – an emotion of love and sorrow interwoven – a carving out of self to make space for God and an urgent though gentle longing to respond to God through better living his live in the service of others.

It is an experience that engenders greater humility because one can never respond in a way that measures up to the gift.

It makes one pray for love and grace.

> Take me into your depths, Lord,
> Take all that I am
> Use me completely as you will
> I give myself into your service.
>
> Leave me only your love and your grace
> that is enough for me
>
> – that is enough,
> more than enough for me.
>
> Take me into your depths, Lord
>   into your heart.
> With Christ
> the delight and passion of my life
>
> deep within.

Chapter 14

LOVE

Returning to Norfolk at the age of fifty made me look again at my roots, for I was born in Norfolk and spent my childhood in Norwich. Going back to the site of the house where I lived until the age of five, I realised that the house, long demolished, would have been only a few hundred yards from the cell of Mother Julian.

It is Julian who comes to mind as I write about love – Julian who sees us as God's darlings and who knew, despite her suffering, that God's meaning is love. Love lies at the heart of our relationship with God, that tender love in which God enfolds and holds us, the love with which he gazes at us as Teresa says 'lovingly and humbly'.

If there has been one thing that has sustained my faith over a lifetime it has not been solely the church, or doctrine, prayer, good people or any sense of self-worth – though these have all played their part. It is simply a fundamental belief in a God of tender love and passionate desire who calls us to himself. It is summed up in a single verse from the Song of Solomon, 'I am my beloved's, and his desire is for me' (7:10).

As was made clear in Chapter 13, being inflamed with love for God may result in 'a sense of piercing beauty – an emotion of love and sorrow interwoven – a carving out of self to make space for God and an urgent though gentle longing to respond to God through better living his live in the service of others'. It is not a selfish love looking only for its own comfort and protection. It is an outgoing love, flowing from our relationship with a loving God.

One of the great insights that came to me as a result of doing the spiritual exercises of St Ignatius was the suggestion that one should stand, before prayer, for the space of an 'Our Father', simply pondering how God our Lord is looking at us. It is standing in this loving gaze of God that I most become my true self. As Anita Burrows writes, 'We are because we are seen; we are because we are loved. The world is because it is beheld and loved into being.'[1]

We are because we are seen

The people in my life who have revealed the face of love are the people who have enabled me to be truly myself. Somehow, in the gaze of love we cannot but help be ourselves – we open up to love and dare to be true. All that time parents waste gazing at a newborn should teach us that gazing with love is never time wasted – it is what creates the roots of trust in a world which, without love, can seem only fearful.

All of us, but especially those of us short on the basic trust which may be gained in childhood, need the gaze of love in an adult world – we need mutual right relationships where we can gaze and be gazed at with love. It is these relationships that facilitate healing and growth. Above all, we may find this mutual relationship of love with God.

My own experience has been that I have often lived in fear. What overcame that pattern was simply coming to a place where I felt myself loved by God, loved to the very core of my being. So when life is tough I come before God and may feel, hear, see nothing but trust that the love I have known is still there and will hold me until I can feel it again. Love has done its work. It has created the trust that carries me between the experiences of love. This is a major source of healing. What was not gained in childhood becomes a learnt pattern of adult faith. God is there gazing at me with love – all the time and in every place. And his love takes me to deep silence and overflowing gratitude. No wonder, then, that so much of my prayer, even in difficult times, begins with an involuntary and constant phrase 'My God I love you', knowing that my love for him is itself a sign of grace – a response to the love with which I am loved. His is the first love.

It is in his gaze that we are loved and in the gaze of the Trinity alone that we are seen as we truly are.

> I need to consider what They think of me. Can I accept that They love me unconditionally, just as I am? Can I accept

that I can come to the Table shabby, worn out and ashamed, and that I will find Them looking on me 'lovingly and humbly', as Saint Teresa says. Can I allow each of Them in turn to kiss me and hug me with joy, as the father does in the parable of the Prodigal Son?

There are two stories of me: Theirs and mine. Mine is built up over the years from what others say of me and what I say of myself. As the years go on, the less appealing it may become. Then there is Their story of me. It began before the world was made, when I was chosen to live through love in Their presence. It is full of hope and stretches out into a limitless and glorious future. It becomes better and better, even as I move into old age, and death looms up. To Them I am no ordinary mortal; I am immortal and totally precious. I must listen to Their story of myself rather than my own. I must pray for the grace to listen well to what the most significant Persons in my life are trying to tell me. Then, also, I can listen to what They say about my neighbours, rather than linger on my story of them.[2]

It is in this gaze of God that I might find the tender love which is flowing eternally between the persons of the Trinity. Indeed, one insight of theology is that in the 'perichoretic' relationship between Father, Son and Spirit, it is the gaze of love between them which makes each more truly who they are. They are held in being by the love they have for each other. Each gives and receives love.

At the heart of the Trinity it is the gaze of love that inspires all that holds us in life and seeks to labour with us in bringing the Kingdom into fruition.

But there is another gaze too – the way that we gaze at God, looking at Jesus the man and finding deep humanity but also the way to divinity. In gazing at him we become more and more like that which we contemplate. We become Christ-like and in becoming Christ-like we become more human and more truly ourselves.

Nor is this just an individual journey, for we cannot gaze at God alone and he at us. He gazes at all his children and we might find him there – in people around us. And when we gaze at others we can gaze with love. We can be God's instruments in helping them become the people that they are created to be – loved, forgiven and free. And the least likely person can be the one who helps us to become who we are meant to be.

As we noticed earlier, Gerard Manley Hopkins writes,

> Christ plays in ten thousand places,
> Lovely in limbs, and lovely in eyes not his,
> To the Father through the features of men's faces.

Christ plays in ten thousand places. It's a lovely line, the outcome of a deep contemplation of God and of other people, seeing Christ in the other, greeting him there with reverence and awe even if in the other he is in the guise of the person we least like, or find it hardest to serve. Contemplation draws us to see Christ trans-figured, not only in our solitude and prayer but in the corridors of our home and workplace, in the street and in the market place.

In practice it means that we can never be self-sufficient. We need other people. There is a mutuality in love through which we will find the healing and growth we so desire. We come back to that gaze of love – and the need in prayer and in life to know that gaze. Of all the words that have helped me pray, perhaps some words of Edwina Gateley are among the most used. She writes:

> Be silent.
> Be still.
> Alone.
> Empty.
> Before your God.
> Say nothing.
> Ask nothing.
> Be silent.
> Be still.
> Let your God look upon you.
> That is all.
> God knows,
> God understands.
> God loves you
> With an enormous love,
> And only wants
> To look upon you
> With that love.

Quiet.
Still.
Be.
Let your God
Love you.[3]

So often, simply sitting with these words have brought perspective back to my life, reminding me that God is a God of love who simply longs to be with us and love us. There is a human aspect to this loving too. It is this – that we need to make time to nurture ourselves by being with people who love us simply for ourselves.

We are because we are loved

'I am my beloved's, and his desire is for me' has become a fundamental text for me. God not only loves me as an artist might love a piece of her work. God desires me. He wants to be in intimate relationship with me – and with you.

What makes that desire so apparent is my own desire and the recognition that inside my desire God is desiring. He is, as Maria Boulding says, 'on the inside of my longing'[4] so that this desire we allow to surface for God is only a reflection of God's *passionate* desire for us. He calls us to himself with an attractive and tender love, longing for us to be his people and himself to be our God – a constant refrain throughout the Old Testament. This desire cannot be overestimated. Rowan Williams goes so far as to say,

> . . . God desires us, *as if we were God*, as if we were that unconditional response to God's giving that God's self makes in the Trinity. We are created so that we may be caught up in this; so that we may grow into the wholehearted love of God by learning that God loves us as God loves God.[5]

God loves us, gazes at us as God gazes at himself – as the Father gazes at the Son and the Son at the Father. He desires us with the desire he desires himself. Here is the heart of my life and prayer and it lies nowhere else but at the heart of the Trinity. My life and prayer, my very heart, is not mine. It is God's.

There is also a living out of love with other people, which helps us understand this fundamental love. Life is a crucible in which the passions of our love and desires find their transformation, often through pain and struggle but also with joy and delight. To be true to experience most human love is imperfect – mine, I sometimes think, more than most. We still bear the scars, however mild, of childhood and they affect the way we love others. Then there are the more obvious scars of adulthood – particularly for those of us who have been widowed or divorced or had a strong relationship break up seemingly beyond our control. These scars are not just those inflicted on us, of course. There are also the scars we have inflicted on others.

How easy it is to seek comfort for ourselves as though we were called to a stultifying peace which deadens us to the pain of life but also to new life. My own experience is more about a spirituality of risk – of daring to love again. Only in risking relationship can I grow in love.

So I have to believe in God's forgiveness as well as his love. How often have I returned to that well-known picture by Rembrandt of the return of the Prodigal Son. Each time I hear again Nouwen's words: 'Had I myself ever dared to step into the centre, kneel down and let myself be held by a forgiving God?'[6] I find myself responding,

> I have to kneel before the Father
>   put my ear against his chest
>   and listen, without interruption to the heartbeat of
>   God . . .
>
> then and only then can I say gently what I hear . . .
>
> and as I kneel, wrapped in his arms, I know myself
>   in Jesus' place – closest to the Father's heart
> I am in Jesus
> and Jesus in me
> this is my calling . . . to be in the Father's arms and heart.
>
> I will set out and go back to my Father.

This is the tender love of God, the love that draws us back to himself and in so doing forgives us and draws us back to our true selves. Here is the Father reminding us that we cannot, simply cannot, do it alone. We need the Father's compassion, to recognise our need for him, in order to take the risk of loving not just once, but again and again.

It is in this twofold movement – of God reaching beyond himself in forgiving us and we reaching beyond ourselves to forgive others and to accept forgiveness – that we grow spiritually. Otherwise we remain captive to our hurts and wounds, those inflicted and those received.

So love does not allow us to stay 'unforgiven'. God reaches beyond himself to draw us back and then, freely, sends us out to love again. And to keep on loving when life seems impossible stretches our hearts as we discover that despite our faults we are capable of a love greater than we imagined.

This ability to love when life seems impossible is another reaching beyond ourselves.

It is not surprising then, that looking back, I realise that much of my own spiritual growth took place during the five years of caring for Jackie and then in the years afterwards reflecting on that experience. When we love and are loved we find ourselves growing in stature in love. Donald Nicholl makes the same observation as he writes about his father's dying:

> Just before I left home, my sister said that she could not understand how I had managed to go on sitting beside my father all the day long and into the night in that cold bedroom and then sleeping for only a few hours on the floor of the room below. There is nothing surprising in that, because you feel you can manage anything when you are serving someone you love with all your heart.[7]

If this is true of human love, and I am convinced it is, how much more is it true of our relationship with God. Pedro Arrupe SJ writes,

> Nothing is more practical than finding God, that is, than falling in love in a quite absolute, final way.
>
> What you are in love with, what seizes your imagination, will affect everything. It will decide what will get you out of bed in the morning, what you do with your evening,

how you spend your weekends, what you read, who you know, what breaks your heart, and what amazes you with joy and gratitude.

Fall in love, stay in love and it will decide everything.[8]

Here we come to the heart of the matter – allowing ourselves to fall in love or be in love with God is central to the spiritual life. It is from that being in love that we find the grace to live the life that is most true to our natures and most true to God.

The world is because it is beheld and loved into being

In writing this I am aware that I am focusing very much on the individual and prayer but there is, of course, another side to all this – that what is true for us is also true for everyone else, and also true of creation itself. We are made by, through and in love.

A response to that love can never just be on the level of the individual. We are involved in creation's longing for freedom – in the struggle for justice throughout the world and in the concern and care for the creation which sustains us in being. This too is prayer. This too is love.

Love in this guise learns much from the teaching of St Ignatius. He writes,

> Love consists in a mutual communication between the two persons. That is, the one who loves gives and communicates to the beloved what he or she has, or a part of what one has or can have; and the beloved in turn does the same to the lover. Thus, if the one has knowledge, one gives it to the other who does not, and similarly in regard to honours or riches. Each shares with the other.[9]

He also writes, 'Love ought to manifest itself more by deeds than by words.'[10]

In these two perceptions Ignatius underlines the meaning and purpose of relationship. In relationship there is mutual sharing in deeds as well as words – and in this we find spiritual growth.

In our relationships with other people on an individual level, and in the search for justice, prayer is revealed through a love which is mutual – ready to give and receive with the kind of generosity which will be explored in Chapter 15.

Creation also needs our generosity – both in our gaining from its inherent wisdom and in our appreciation, enjoyment and practical nurturing of its resources.

Chapter 15

GROWING INTO CHRIST

I HAVE BEEN WAITING TO WRITE THIS CHAPTER FOR MONTHS. The right moment never seemed to come. Then I found myself ready. God had taken me back into the depths of pain and love which is always, for me, the place of insight, growth and transformation. Now, in this place, I can talk of the transformation of the soul which lies at the heart of much of what I have written about prayer.

We need to look at this combination of love and pain, and at the inner attitude of generosity which allows it to happen. Then we shall look at three different ways in which growth may happen.

Love and pain

It has always seemed to me that love and pain lie close together, especially when God is at work in the soul. God draws us, attracts us, by love but the transformation of the soul is like being touched by fire; the dross has to be burnt away until the soul, transfigured by fire, burns with the fire of God's love.

I am writing this while staying at St Beuno's Spirituality Centre in North Wales, an Ignatian retreat house. In my mind, not surprisingly, is the figure of Ignatius of Loyola and his *Spiritual Exercises*. But alongside him is another great saint who has also spoken profoundly to my life and love – St John of the Cross.

The spiritual exercises of St Ignatius, which have so touched my spiritual formation, are almost impossible to describe in terms of the effect they have on a person who is open to that encounter with God which the exercises provoke. In my own experience, and in accompanying others (either through the thirty-day retreat or through doing the exercises in everyday life), I have seen how the exercises take us from a superficial knowledge of God and his love to a deep heartfelt knowledge, which not only strengthens and consoles the person but inspires them to serve Christ by serving the needs of the world. The strong image I have from the exercises is of a contemplation placed near the end, called the 'Contemplatio'. It often forms part of the so-called 'fourth week' of the exercises and in it we catch a glimpse of the all-pervading love of God. I have prayed through the exercises twice and each time this part of them has brought me to a depth of love which actually hurts. It was by chance that glancing though a book about Gerard Manley Hopkins I came across a passage which best describes my experience:

> One after one the outer casings of consciousness are stripped off until the penitent touches the nerve and quick of consciousness, until all else falls away into illimitable darkness, until he is alone in the white light of a unique and central ecstasy, of a love so ardent that it exhausts the power of loving. This, then, should he discover it, is the true meaning of his calling. This is to be with God. This is to be of God.[1]

More prosaically I found myself writing:

> Stillness.
> Silence, as if
> as if the world had stopped turning
> as if the sea no longer swayed
> nor the stars sang their way across the sky.
> Deep silence within
> refreshing the soul.
> Enfolding in love
> somehow connecting
> engaging the soul with God.
> The pain? It's still real
> the exhaustion complete
> but this is beyond both
> deeper and broader.
> Somehow all is held
> embraced, enveloped

within a love
that draws me to a single point
a union
a desire for more
GOD.

The second strong image is from the writings of St John of the Cross. He describes how God comes to the soul like a fire:

> The very fire of love that afterward is united with the soul, glorifying it, is what previously assailed it by purging it, just as the fire that penetrates a log of wood is the same that makes an assault on the wood, wounding it with the flame, drying it out, and stripping it of its unsightly qualities until it is so disposed that it can be penetrated and transformed into the fire.[2]

In both these images there is love and pain. In finding a breakthrough we may experience seeming breakdown. William Johnston describes it succinctly:

> this . . . is a time of death and resurrection. The framework that upheld one's life collapses leaving one adrift on a sea of insecurity. But in the midst of this turmoil comes a call . . . One is called to something new.[3]

What is God doing? He is re-creating us. In the words of St Bernard, 'In the first creation God gave me myself. In the second creation he gave me himself and so restored to me the self that I had lost.'

Whether it is through the Ignatian exercises or through experiencing the 'dark night' of John's understanding, the effect on me is the same: God is stripping me down to the self that he has made, asking me to accept his wisdom in making me 'me' and inviting me to surrender all of that self to his service.

And when I find myself at this point of the journey three prayers come to my lips: the prayers of Ignatius[4] and of Charles de Foucauld and a prayer which has been inspired by both.[5] De Foucauld writes:

> My Father, I abandon myself to you.
> Do with me as you will.

Whatever you may do with me I thank you.
I am prepared for anything. I accept everything,
provided your will is fulfilled in me and in all creatures.
I ask for nothing more, my God.
I place my soul in your hands.
I give it to you, my God,
with all the love of my heart,
because I love you.
And for me it is a necessity of love,
this gift of myself,
this placing of myself in your hands
without reserve
in boundless confidence
because you are my Father.

What inspires these words? Love and love alone. Only when they are spoken from love, by love, in response to love do they become surrender . . . and the love is not ours – love that has been wrought from wound-up courage and gritted teeth. It is a different love. It is the love in which God holds the soul . . . almost a physical sense of God holding the heart in tenderness and joy.

All we can do is cultivate an attitude of generosity.

Generosity

It is only recently that I have come to better understand what generosity is in the Christian life. I had, long ago, been inspired by a story told by Mother Teresa of Calcutta. She had heard someone ask an Indian gentleman what it meant to be a Christian. He had replied, 'It's a giving, it's a giving . . .' I have returned to the story again and again encouraging myself to be more generous, to keep giving.

But now I have understood generosity far more in the light of that monk we quoted in Chapter 4 – generosity as giving God access: 'your entire availability'[6] to God. This is true, too, to the Ignatian exercises' understanding of generosity, which is much more about being prepared to let God work on the soul. True generosity is to be open and receptive to God – not so much a giving as a receiving and a willingness to be changed by God. It is precisely what is needed if we are to be transformed by God ever more into his likeness. In these prayers I find myself dwelling on the lines, 'do with it what you will. Give me only your LOVE and your GRACE', 'Do with me as you will. Whatever you may do I thank you. I am prepared for anything. I accept everything' and 'Use me completely as you will.' It is here that we see generosity, or to use another of Mother Teresa's favoured words, it is here that we put ourselves at God's *disposal*, allowing God to sculpt us into his work of art.

So God changes us. And if the cost is high, alongside it the love is deep. The journey is only possible because the loving God is in it too – and as those words from Jeremiah 29 remind us, God has plans.

> For surely I know the plans I have for you, says the LORD, plans for your welfare and not for harm, to give you a future with hope. Then when you call upon me and come and pray to me, I will hear you. When you search for me, you will find me; if you seek me with all your heart, I will let you find me, says the LORD. (Jeremiah 29:11-14)[7]

As we saw in Chapter 2, those words became very important when Jackie was ill. They reassured me, comforted me. I thought that when Jackie died nothing much else could happen. In fact, the past fifteen years have contained plenty of trauma. Life has not got easier. When I read these verses again recently I was surprised that I was not angry. What was all this about a future and a hope? Then I reflected on the rest of the verses: 'When you search for me, you will find me; if you seek me with all your heart.'

When Jackie died I knew I had found God far more deeply as a result of that period of suffering. I set out to find him also in the rest of life, in joy and glory. Looking back, my knowledge of God, my desire for him and my love for him have all deepened over these years: 'I will let you find me, says the LORD.'

Somehow God has used all the experience of those years – a long period of depression, divorce and enormous inner turmoil as well as calmer times, to draw me to himself. His generosity has made up for my lack of generosity, his love used the chisel blows of life to make caverns of space in me that only he can fill.

Am I embarrassed by claiming this? Yes, and no. 'Yes', because I never imagined writing it down for others to read, but the desire has grown to write a book on prayer that tells it as it is. 'No' because I know from what others say that they see something of God which I know not to be attributable to my own goodness but can only be a gift and yes, I am embarrassed by God's generosity, but happily so.

Growth

Iain Matthew suggests that John of the Cross 'sees the world slung between Friday and Sunday – a dying and rising where all have a home'.[8] This evocative image of the world being caught within the transforming power of the Paschal mystery is at the root of my understanding of the change that happens in those who seek God. On reflection I have noticed three ways of understanding growth – being held in love, spontaneous gift and the scouring of love and pain.

Being held in love

We talked in Chapter 14 of God's gaze of love – something which both Ignatius and John of the Cross understand as crucial. John writes:

> When God looks, he loves and grants favours.[9]
> When you looked at me
> your eyes imprinted your grace in me[10]
> It should be known that God's gaze produces four
>   goods in the soul. It cleanses, endows with grace,
>   enriches and illumines . . . [11]

This gaze of love is not only the love we find in becoming aware of God looking at us, but is also the love we meet in life when we encounter people who offer us love which is unconditional, self-giving, warm, generous, creative, gentle and empathetic. Above all these words I would put one other – tender. To return to John of the Cross, he begins his poem 'The Living Flame of Love' with the words,

> O living flame of love
> that *tenderly* wounds my soul
> in its deepest centre! Since
> now you are not oppressive,

> now consummate! If it be your will:
> tear through the veil of this sweet encounter![12]

and finishes it,

> how *tenderly* you swell my heart with love.[13]

Then, in the text he writes,

> Since this flame is a flame of divine life, it wounds the soul
> with the *tenderness* of God's life, and it wounds and stirs it
> so deeply as to make it dissolve in love.[14]

What do we experience when we experience this tenderness in another person? I know of no better description than that given by the person-centred therapist Brian Thorne. He defines tenderness as:

> In the first place it is a quality which irradiates the total
> person – it is evident in the voice, the eyes, the hands, the
> thoughts, the feelings, the beliefs, the moral stance, the
> attitude to things animate and inanimate, seen and unseen.
> Secondly, it communicates through its responsive vulnera-
> bility that suffering and healing are interwoven. Thirdly, it
> demonstrates a preparedness and an ability to move
> between the worlds of the physical, the emotional, the
> cognitive and the mystical without strain. Fourthly, it is
> without shame because it is experienced as the joyful
> embracing of the desire to love and it is therefore a law
> unto itself. Fifthly, it is a quality which transcends the male
> and female but is nevertheless nourished by the attraction
> of the one for the other in the quest for wholeness.[15]

When somebody offers us tenderness they are making God near for us. We cannot help but grow into the person we are meant to be.

I believe this kind of growth lies at the heart of creation, indeed at the heart of a God within whom, as Trinity, there is the tenderness of infinite love.

Spontaneous gift

If the world is slung between Good Friday and Easter then it has the possibility of Paschal growth – growth which is unexpected and surprising. There is no parallel for what happened at the resurrection. Images of eggs, of butterflies, of peacocks have all been used but they all reflect a steady growth, which appears dramatic but is written in the genes. Resurrection is not. It is of a different order. Sometimes we are taken out of life into death and into new life. It is this kind of growth that John of the Cross is so keen to describe – those periods in life when we are bewildered by what is happening to us and enter what feels like oblivion before we can see where we are going. What is important in these times is not just that they are happening. On their own they can be, and are frequently, destructive. What matters is that alongside bewilderment there is an in-breaking of God and a response from the person who is experiencing such a time.

As I reflect on my own life I am struck by how, in times of distress, my sense of God's love has grown, love for God has deepened and I have found myself wanting to say 'Yes' with all of me. At one such time I wrote:

> All I am is love before God
> my whole being
> crying 'Yes'.
> Let it be dear Lord.
> Let it be to me
> according to your word.
> Let it be to me
> you, not me,
> who acts.
> Let it be
> you, not me
> who speaks.
> Let it be you
> not me
> you, only you
> you holding me, filling me,
> using me,

laying me aside
totally available
needing your touch
your life.

Life had taken me to a place of seeming oblivion. So here, at the bottom, I recognise that I can do nothing. Only God can make this happen – this new birth, new life. It is here that the Paschal mystery takes hold in our lives – when we are taken to seeming death and find instead new life.

A few days later, still waiting, I wrote

All I am
is stillness before God
empty, waiting to be filled,
songless, waiting for a song
a violin string
waiting for the bow.
Deep stillness.
Hush,
the soul is waiting for her God
longingly,
lovingly
gently
tenderly
waiting at a window
for her lover.

Looking back at that period I am amazed by the depth of love and seeming calmness in what I remember as an excruciatingly painful time.

This Paschal growth does not necessarily happen only from a place of pain (though that has been my experience) but may be that sense of being surprised by joy even when passing through seemingly tranquil times.

The scouring of love and pain

Donald Nicholl argues that there is no exclusive *locus* for theology but that, following the example of St Paul, our *locus* should be one where we are constantly ready for dislocation: '. . . because it is only by being dislocated that one is enabled to see and to witness to the truths of our faith'.[16] So I am writing from that place – a sense of dislocation. It is from this perspective that I turn again and again to the writing of Simone Weil:

> God created through love and for love. God did not create anything but love itself, and the means to love. He created love in all its forms. He created beings capable of love from all possible distances. Because nobody other could do it, he himself went to the greatest possible distance, the infinite distance. This infinite distance between God and God, this supreme tearing apart, this agony beyond all others, this marvel of love, is the crucifixion. Nothing can be further from God than that which has been made accursed.
>
> This tearing apart over which supreme love places the bond of supreme union, echoes perpetually across the universe in the midst of the silence, like two notes, separate and yet melting into one, like pure and heartrending harmony. This is the Word of God. The whole of creation is nothing but its vibration . . . those who persevere in love hear this note from the very lowest depths into which affliction has thrust them. From that moment they can no longer have any doubt.[17]

The tension between love and pain has already been explored earlier in the chapter and the tenderness of love seen as part of what enables growth to happen. In suggesting that love and pain can scour us – cleansing us and making space for God – I am in no way glorifying suffering. We need to understand what this 'pain' is. It is the pain which we carry simply because we are who we are and because we are seeking to follow Christ.[18] It is not the whole of that pain either. It is the residual pain, when we have alleviated all that we can without being false either to our true selves or to God.

Such a pain has been with me as I write this chapter. My journal reads,

> I am amazed – I came last evening talking of the pain of the last few weeks and also of a sense of God's love . . . but the veil between the two has been thin – I have walked from

the depths of pain to the depths of love . . . from skinless
painful vulnerability to ecstasy . . . with nothing between
the two and with no need to come out of one to go into the
other . . . there is interconnection at depth.

And the outcome? A deepening sense of God's love, a recognition
that the pain is real and needs to be addressed, and a greater trust
that this, too, is part of the journey.

It is especially at times such as these that being accompanied by
a wise spiritual director is essential. They may only be able to sit
alongside, but in reflecting the tender love of God they are con-
tributing to the necessary healing – providing a safe place where we
are held, and a safeguard against self-delusion.

His meaning is love

In these three ways of growing (which overlap and inter-relate) God
is simply attracting the soul and so the whole person into an
ever-deepening relationship with himself. As we have noted, the
accompaniment of another may be crucial if God is working at this
depth in our journey. It is to this that we turn in the final chapter.

Chapter 16

BETWEEN FIRE AND WATER

THIS BOOK IS AN ODD SORT OF BOOK. It is not methodical, nor does it teach about prayer from any particular standpoint, though it will be clear that I am heavily indebted both to Ignatius of Loyola and St John of the Cross. There are a number of other profound influences from the tradition which have been formative in my understanding – notably Julian of Norwich, Francis de Sales, Jane de Chantal, St Benedict, Mother Mary Clare SLG and others. Writing it has been purely an exercise in reflecting on prayer and an exercise in prayer itself. What has surprised me has been to note the particular importance of my many times of retreat. The other major factor in my understanding of myself as someone who prays has been having a spiritual director alongside me to accompany me.

In this chapter, written from the heart of prayer, we explore these two influences – retreats and spiritual direction.

In fact, I am writing this final chapter soon after my most recent, eight-day silent retreat. What has emerged from this retreat has been the recognition that my love of John of the Cross probably derives from what Iain Matthew says of him – 'He was exposed to life's open wounds and was formed by that experience',[1] 'a youth forged by love and pain'.[2] My journey, too, has been about being scoured by love and pain as described in Chapter 15. I am encouraged, then, by Iain Matthew, who goes on to suggest that all of us can share John's vision even if our experience is less extreme.

Certainly my own experience of looking after Jackie opened up vistas of love and pain I had never expected to know. Now, fifteen years on, I see what has happened to me. Caught between love and pain I plummeted to the depths of my being and to the depths and heights of God's love. Ever since then I have been trying to understand the profundity and gift of the experience.

As a result of this and other life experiences there has opened up a clash of contraries – I know immense love and immense pain. Both can feel too much to bear at times and yet they have 'scoured me' and opened me up to God. A particular passage from the Apocrypha has twice spoken to this condition. It is 2 Esdras 7:3-9:

> I said, 'Speak, my lord.' And he said to me, 'There is a sea set in a wide expanse so that it is deep and vast, but it has an entrance set in a narrow place, so that it is like a river. If there are those who wish to reach the sea, to look at it or to navigate it, how can they come to the broad part unless they pass through the narrow part? Another example: There is a city built and set on a plain, and it is full of all good things; but the entrance to it is narrow and set in a precipitous place, so that there is fire on the right hand and deep water on the left. There is only one path lying between them, that is, between the fire and the water, so that only one person can walk on the path. If now the city is given to someone as an inheritance, how will the heir receive the inheritance unless by passing through the appointed danger?'

Both fire and water have become powerful images. Fire representing the fire of God's love, which breaks down my resistance, cleanses me, and is a mark of his intimate approach. It also represents the scorching that sometimes seems to come my way from life and the hurt I have done to others. Water represents something deeply profound which wells up in me – the kind of living water of John 7:38-39. For me it is most beautifully expressed by a visit to St Winifred's well in Holywell. There the water quietly rises to the surface of the pool – a constant but gentle renewing source of life.

God's love refreshes me too. But there is another side to water. Sometimes, when life is too much, it is like being sucked under. It's something I have known and which found articulation when I read Elie Wiesel's *All Rivers Run to the Sea*. He writes,

> A sadness as deep as the ocean enveloped me, so oppressive that I found it hard to breathe, so powerful that I had a sudden urge to throw myself overboard and be swallowed up and carried off by the waters.[3]

Somehow I need to gather the gifts of these images and avoid that
which is destructive about them. The passage from 2 Esdras speaks,
for me, to this situation. The path between fire and water is only
wide enough for one person. As I pray, that person is Christ. Along
the path I imagine the words from the Song of Songs, 'You are
beautiful my love, altogether lovely.' It is in walking at one with
him that I may safely traverse fire and water and find that which I
desire – union with God.

> Shoulder wide
> this path I tread.
> Shoulder wide
> mine or his?
> Beauty, Jesus is before me,
> end of my path
> but also within me
> love of my life
> and there beneath me
> my earth
> and there above me
> my air
> there beside me
> in fire of passion
> and water of life.
> No fear now,
> calm, still, be
> JESUS
> the path I desire
> the 'rest' that has eluded me
> the everything
> that greets my nothing.
> Caught in your gaze
> water wells up –
> overflowing once more
> as wounding with love
> your flame anoints me.

As we will see at the end of the chapter this image of fire has been
with me for a long time – it is a fire nurtured by prayer – prayer that

has been shared with a spiritual director and often has been experienced most profoundly on retreat.

Having a spiritual director

When I review my life I realise that my own commitment to the spiritual life and to prayer took a major change of direction when I found a spiritual director who could empathise with my journey and help me to understand my prayer and life *as one*. They provided a 'safe' space where confidentiality was assured, where I felt totally accepted, and where the time was clearly given over to looking at what God might be doing in my life. This almost defines spiritual direction. It is the accompaniment of one person by another with the intention of helping that other to grow spiritually in the way that God leads them to grow. The focus for both people in the spiritual direction relationship is on God. Both are expecting to encounter and follow God through the relationship as through the rest of life.

For years now I have found myself both receiving spiritual direction and offering it for others. It never ceases to amaze me what a difference it makes to have someone in that role. Somehow it gives courage to explore areas of our lives which we might otherwise have compartmentalised and excluded from our life of prayer. In other words, it does precisely what this book is attempting to do: it helps to keep the connections between life and prayer vibrant, meaningful and purposeful.

That's not to say that growth in the spiritual life is necessarily any easier because someone is alongside. It may, indeed, be that the growth they facilitate may mean that we are no longer content with false comfort or religious mediocrity but are prepared to look at what is most real for us and to trust the deeper recesses of our lived experience.

In my own experience it was a particular retreat followed by the accompaniment of a new spiritual director through which God invited me to explore an area of my life which I had foolishly tried to ignore for many years. Exploring it turned my life and the life of others upside down. Throughout that time, though, my knowledge of God's love has deepened immeasurably. The self-knowledge and understanding gained has also meant that I am more available for others – partly because I have a better understanding of the human condition and partly because, knowing myself as I now do, I cannot begin to judge others.

There is a threefold growth here – growth in relationship with God, with self and with others. It has not been an easy time. Any peace I have felt has been at the deeper levels, whilst on the surface have often been swelling seas and windswept oceans' waves. Without having a good spiritual director and good friends I doubt I would have dared stay with the journey.

Going on retreat

Retreats have played a crucial role in my journey through this time.

Retreats come in a number of different forms. When I first went on retreat they were what is called 'preached retreats'. On these retreats there are one or two talks each day. Apart from these, and meals and times of worship, the rest of the day would be free for recreation, relaxation and prayer.

In 1990, after Jackie died, I realised I needed something else and so went on an 'individually guided retreat' (IGR). On these retreats each retreatant is assigned a director. There is a daily meeting between the two so that they can get to know each other and so that the director can listen to the retreatant's experience of life and prayer. Then fresh materials may be provided for prayer for the following period of time. The rest of the day is spent in silence. Often there is a daily Eucharist and in many houses an opportunity to gather for communal silent prayer in the evening.

It was on this kind of retreat that I rediscovered Jesus (or he rediscovered me).

Many of these kinds of retreats take their inspiration from the life and teaching of St Ignatius of Loyola. His original *Spiritual Exercises* were written to be the material for prayer for a thirty-day silent retreat. He also made provision for those who could not do the thirty days, to use the exercises in daily life over a longer period. In my own case that meant a weekly meeting with my director over a period of about nine months. A few years later I did the thirty-day form.

To these two experiences I owe my present life. If the first reaffirmed my vocation to follow Christ, the second reaffirmed my commitment above all to a life of prayer.

Preached retreats and IGRs remain popular forms of retreat.

Alongside them there are a number of 'themed retreats' – where one may explore, for example, art, sculpture or music as inspiration for prayer.

Less well known are 'desert retreats'. My own experience of a desert retreat meant simply going with a group of five others to share a house for a week. No aids for prayer are available – no Scriptures, books, pictures or icons. One is simply left with one's own resources. Not surprisingly, God draws up from memory those texts and images that we can use for prayer. But there is barrenness too and a sense of encountering the God of the desert.

For those who cannot go on retreat there are other ways of getting something of the experience. Certainly, for some, the spiritual exercises of St Ignatius in daily life are a possibility, provided that a knowledgeable and sympathetic director can be found. But there are less rigorous possibilities too. Parishes are increasingly holding weeks of guided prayer, where people come daily to see a director and then commit themselves to praying with the material offered before the next day. There are also a number of groups which meet specifically for prayer and to share the experience of what prayer has been over the preceding period.

A commitment to prayer

One thing is necessary in order to grow in the life of prayer and that is to commit oneself to praying.

I find myself praying in all sorts of places and at all times of day but know that unless I have a committed time each day then I am falling away from my true vocation, which has always been to pray. Childhood memories take me to words from a Lenten hymn, 'while I breathe, I pray', and my thirty-day retreat made this clear. I saw my life, looking back, as having a single common thread – the prayer that God has been praying in me even when I have not been praying. I cannot exist without prayer as the breath of my life.

Almost ten years ago I wrote:

> Fire is risky stuff. Fire consumes. It can destroy. To enter fire is to risk everything. There are no half measures. 'We only live, only suspire, consumed by either fire or fire' (T. S. Eliot). We give our life either to God's consuming fire or to the fire of life without God. It doesn't sound much of a

choice and yet it is. It is to choose between nothingness for its own sake, or the nothingness that leads to the fullness of God – to be consumed by nothing or to be consumed by love.

And it is only when we trust in the love beyond the nothingness that it is safe to enter the fire. It is only love that calls us on, to be, like the butterfly, stripped of our skin and standing skinless in our own pain and inadequacy. Without love it is not possible. *'Things fall apart, the centre cannot hold'* (Yeats). And the love is in the fire. Nobody describes it better that St John of the Cross. At times in the spiritual journey the fire can feel aggressive – *'like fire burning into wood, first making it sputter and steam, blacken and crackle, until the wood itself become flame. But whether the flame is purifying or glorifying, it is the same "fire of love" that is approaching, entering'* (Iain Matthew, *Impact of God*).

When we ask the Spirit to come, to kindle a fire of love, isn't this what we are asking, that the events of life which strike us and shape us may be the means by which the wounds of love are deepened and the veils between us and God torn down. Torn at first with all the pain of the tearing but at times caught up in the flame of love which is the spirit, pierced by nothing but longing love, and that God's longing as well as ours? Isn't this the fire, that we are able to let God surrender himself to us, and we, warmed by his love, so surrender ourselves to him?

The fire is to be in us, his fire alight *'on the mean altar of my heart'*, as Wesley puts it, taking as his image the everlasting fire of Leviticus 6, *'A perpetual fire shall be kept burning on the altar.'* Amen to that, to the fire of love, whether it be purifying or glorifying, to the fire of God's love deep within, to that fire which burns with love and transforms and transfigures all that is offered to its blaze into the love *of* God for others. Amen to burning *'with the love of God so that others do not die of the cold'* (F. Mauriac). Amen to living only for him. Amen to being warmed by the spirit and set free to fly.

It is prayer which has kept me aware of God's fire burning in my soul – fire which has tenderly wounded my heart and joined me deeper and deeper with God. Without prayer I am not alive to the joy of God's presence and to the sense of being one with him.

Breathing, I pray

Prayer, retreats and spiritual direction have brought me to this point. They have made me see that despite my weakness and frailty God can still come to me and take all of me. He and I can be one in this life for fleeting moments but surely one in the next. And that's enough, more than enough for me. But 'this point' is only the beginning. I have tried to capture the essence of my prayer over nearly half a century but I know I have only just begun. Yet, as a beginner, I know myself sometimes, just sometimes, close to the creator of the universe – at home with the living God.

On my hand there is a pewter ring. It tells the story of my prayer.

> Pewter
> so ordinary
> yet joining the extraordinary
> – my God and I.
> Ecstasy of love it was,
> ecstasy in softest silence joined
> my God and I.
> Beautiful we were together
> dusk pink stillness by the sea
> lovers walking
> talking
> joining souls in tender joy.
> A band of pewter around my finger
> is nothing
> like
> his everything
> spangles of gold
> deep within my heart
> where you
> my lover God
> and I
> are one.

POSTSCRIPT

From a sermon preached 13 October 1997

. . . for most of us the suffering is about learning to live with ourselves. For most of us that is the greatest cross we carry. It would be easy to be a Christian if we were not as we are. For most of us the cost is learning to trust that God loves us, not despite our sins but beyond our sin. For most of us the cost is daring to lay down the whole of our lives so that every part is transparent to God. I was talking the other day to some-body convinced that they had somehow to dispose of their past before God would ever accept them fully. As I listened I became aware that in fact their past had developed in them an amazing capacity for compas-sion for others and this was already being used in ministry. Their past didn't need to be disposed of. It needed to be laid down before God so that it too could be consecrated to his purpose. There is nothing about us that God cannot use, only that which has not been laid down before him. You see, he does not commission part of us. He commissions all that we are. He doesn't want us to lay down part of our life. He wants us to lay it all down. So many people I listen to want to leave them-selves at the foot of the cross and become somebody else. It's such a shame. For the cross rose up from the rubbish tip not to point the way to the tip but to transform all our 'rubbish' into glory. In Christ, that which we most despise becomes the stuff of eternity. That which you most dislike about yourself, offered to Christ, laid down in him, will be your greatest gift to Christ's ministry. Now that is the cost. To believe it. To allow Christ to use you – all of you. The cost is great. For some, life will involve physical suffering, torture, persecution, ridicule, death. Yes, the cost is great, but the love is greater.

In the whole of life, whatever you do, wherever you are, Christ is there, standing there, loving you. He is at the head of every avenue, the top of every staircase. He stands there beautiful and attractive, loving you, drawing you to himself with outstretched arms.

Let him love you.

APPENDIX: AN IMAGINATIVE
REVIEW OF THE DAY

Come to stillness in your usual way.

Imagine yourself in a place you know well and in a comfortable chair. Alongside is another chair. Imagine the room/space so that you are comfortably there.

There is a knock on the door and, opening it, you find Jesus there carrying a book. You invite him to sit down. (How does it feel to have him there?) He opens the book and you realise it is a photograph album of the day. There are pictures there from the time you got up right through the day.

You and Jesus look through the photographs, talking about what they are about. If one in particular catches your eye, for which you are grateful – spend some time with that and talk to Jesus about it . . .

Is there a particular picture Jesus wants you to look at? What do you feel about his choice? What will you say to him?

(Maybe there's a picture there which you wish wasn't there. Talk to Jesus about that too.)

When you are ready you close the album, which in fact represents your day, and give it to Jesus. Is there anything else you would like to say to him?

When you have finished talking with Jesus as to a friend then either:

- He gives you an empty album. Inside you find that he has written your name followed by the words, 'With love and grace for tomorrow, Jesus'. How do you feel? What do you say? OR
- He gives you an empty album and you ask him to be with you tomorrow.

Bring this review of the day to a gentle close with a simple prayer and let your day be held by Jesus as you leave your prayer time.

NOTES

1. 'Christian dost thou see them', *Hymns Ancient and Modern Revised* (London: William Clowes and Son).

Chapter 1: REFLECTION AND MEANING
1. John O'Donohue, *Conamara Blues* (London: Doubleday, 2000), p.30.
2. Ivan Mann, *A Double Thirst* (London: DLT, 2001), p.161f.
3. Appendix 1 is another simple way of doing this reflection. I am grateful for the idea for this reflection which came from Mags Blackie.

Chapter 2: CHEWING THE CUD
1. Brian Thorne, *Infinitely Beloved* (London: DLT, 2003).

Chapter 3: PSALMS AND POETRY
1. *New Jerusalem Bible* (London: DLT, 1990).
2. This is a 'desert retreat', described more fully in Chapter 16.
3. Hugo Williams, 'Siren Song' quoted in Foreword, Mariella Frostrup, *The Nation's Favourite Poems of Desire* (London: BBC, 2003), p.110.
4. R. S. Thomas, *Collected Poems 1945–1990* (London: Phoenix Giants, 1993), p.104.
5. Gerard Manley Hopkins, 'The Wreck of the Deutschland', *The Poems of Gerard Manley Hopkins* (London: OUP, 1949), p.55.
6. R. S. Thomas, *Collected Poems 1945–1990* (London: Phoenix Giants, 1993), p.283.
7. Nicholas Wolterstorff, *Lament for a Son* (Michigan: Eerdmans Publishing Company, 2002), p.6.
8. ibid, p.80.

Chapter 4: IMAGINATION
1. Alan Neame, *The Hermitage Within* (London: DLT, 1999).
2. Brian Keenan, *An Evil Cradling* (London: Hutchinson, 1992), p.68f.
3. Maria Boulding, *The Coming of God* (London: Fount, 1984), p.7.
4. Desmond Doig, *Mother Teresa: Her people and her work* (London: Collins, 1976), p.129.

5. Cf. Julian of Norwich, *Revelations of Divine Love*, Chapter 5.

Chapter 5: JESUS PRAYER
1. St Augustine, quoted in Boniface Ramsey, *Beginning to Read the Fathers* (London: DLT, 1987), p.171.

Chapter 6: SILENCE
1. As Kahlil Gibran so helpfully says in *The Prophet* (London: Heinemann, 1976), p.61.
2. Maria Boulding, *The Coming of God* (London: SPCK, 1982), p.37.
3. This image is further explored in Chapter 15.
4. Rubem A. Alves *The Poet, The Warrior, The Prophet* (London: SCM, 2002), p.28.

Chapter 7: CREATION AND CREATIVITY
1. Ian McEwan, *Amsterdam* (London: QPD, 1999), p.24.
2. Further source unknown.
3. C. Day Lewis, *The Complete Poems* (London: Sinclair-Stevenson, 1992), p.734.
4. Osip Mandelstam, *Selected Poems* (London: Penguin, 1991), p.36.

Chapter 8: MUSIC
1. The rest of this poem is quoted in Ivan Mann, *A Double Thirst* (London: DLT, 2001), p.148f.
2. Cf. John of the Cross: it should be known that God's gaze produces four goods in the soul: It cleanses, endows with grace, enriches and illumines, like the sun that dries and provides warmth and beauty and splendour when it pours down its rays. (Canticle 33.1).
3. Sr Wendy Beckett, *Art and the Sacred* (London: Rider, 1992), p.7f.
4. Pro Corda. See also page 113.
5. See Chapter 13.

Chapter 9: EUCHARIST
1. Quoted in Michele Guinness, *Tapestry of Voices* (London, Triangle, 1993), p.51.
2. Christopher Nolan, *Under the Eye of the Clock* (London: Weidenfield and Nicolson, 1987), p.60.
3. See p.43.
4. See p.117.

Chapter 10: STUDY AND SCRIPTURE
1. Cf. the Two Standard exercise.
2. *The Wound of Love: A Carthusian Miscellany* (London: DLT, 1994), p.55.

3. Kenneth Leech, *Spirituality and Pastoral Care* (London: Sheldon, 1986), p.7.
4. *Spiritual Exercises* [103].

Chapter 11: CONNECTEDNESS WITH HUMANITY

1. Richard Cleaver, *Know My Name* (Louisville: Westminster John Knox Press, 1995), p.80.
2. Meister Eckhart (c.1260-1327).
3. Source unknown.

Chapter 12: MYSELF

1. Thomas Mann, *Death in Venice, Tristan, Tonio Kroger* (Harmondsworth: Penguin Modern Classics, 1985), p.29.
2. Quoted in Felicitas Corrigan, *A Benedictine Tapestry* (London: DLT, 1991), p.126.
3. Bishop Theophan the Recluse, quoted in Kallistos Ware, *The Power of the Name* (Oxford: Fairacres Publicatons, 1986).
4. Quoted in Mother Mary Clare, *Learning to Pray* (Oxford: SLG Press, 1970).
5. Ed. Ivan Mann, *The Golden Key* (Northampton: Motor Neurone Disease Association, 1990), p.80.

Chapter 13: TEARS

1. Philip Caraman, *Ignatius Loyola* (London: Collins, 1990), p.159.
2. See, e.g., Kyriacos C. Markides, *The Mountain of Silence* (London: Doubleday, 2002), p.90, 'He just felt this exquisite sweetness when he prayed to Christ with tears in his eyes. But his parents became deeply concerned. They thought his behaviour was abnormal.'
3. Margaret Magdalen CSMV, *Furnace of the Heart* (London: DLT, 1998), p.65.
4. Pro Corda, based at Leiston Abbey in Suffolk.
5. Cf. St John Climacus remarked that true beauty is never profane: 'When we hear singing,' he said, 'let us be moved with love towards God; for those who love God are touched with a holy joy, a divine emotion and tenderness which brings them to tears when they listen to beautiful harmony, *whether the songs are sacred or profane.*' The Ladder, 15th step, quoted in Olivier Clement, *On Human Being* (London: New City, 2000), p.105f.
6. Inversnaid, *Poems of Gerard Manley Hopkins* (Oxford: OUP, 1949), p.95.
7. Daniel Bedingfield.
8. Vanessa Herrick and Ivan Mann, *Jesus Wept* (London: DLT, 1998).

Chapter 14: LOVE

1. Trans. Anita Burrows and Joanna Macy, *Rilke's Book of Hours* (New York: Riverhood Books, 1996), p.15.
2. Sr Una O'Connor IBVM and Fr Brian Grogan SJ, *Love Beyond all telling* (Dublin: Irish Messenger Publications, 1988), p.43f.
3. Edwina Gateley, *Psalms of a Laywoman* (Wisconsin: Sheed and Ward, 1998), p.59.
4. Maria Boulding, *The Coming of God* (London: SPCK, 1961), p.7.
5. Rowan Williams, *The Body's Grace* (London: LGCM, 2002), p.3.
6. Henri J. M. Nouwen, *The Return of the Prodigal Son* (London: DLT, 1992,), p.11.
7. Donald Nicholl, *The Testing of Hearts* (London: DLT, 1998), p.13.
8. Pedro Arrupe SJ, further source unknown.
9. George E. Ganss, *The Spiritual Exercises of Saint Ignatius* (Chicago: Loyola Press, 1992), p.94.
10. ibid.

Chapter 15: GROWING INTO CHRIST

1. Eleanor Ruggles, *Gerard Manley Hopkins: A Life* (London: John Lane Bodley Head, 1947), p.85.
2. Trans. Kieran Kavanaugh OCD and Otilio Rodriguez OCD, *Collected Works of St John of the Cross* (Washington D.C.: ICS Publications, 1991), p.648.
3. William Johnston, *Being in Love* (London: Fount, 1988), p.89.
4. Quoted in Chapter 8. See p.69.
5. The concluding prayer of Chapter 13.
6. Alan Neame, *The Hermitage Within* (London: DLT, 1999), p.10.
7. Iain Matthew says of St John of the Cross: John does not want to say, 'It's all right, you see, because this is the explanation.' He wants to say, 'It's not all right, it's a mess. But you are not alone in this. God is present in this. Now is not the time to lose faith in him.' Iain Matthew, *Impact of God* (London: Hodder and Stoughton, 1995), p.85.
8. Iain Matthew, *The Impact of God* (London: Hodder and Stoughton, 1995), p.2.
9. *Collected Works*, p.551 (Canticle 19.6).
10. *Collected Works*, p.599 (Canticle 32).
11. *Collected Works*, p.601 (Canticle 33.1).
12. *Collected Works*, p.643 (Living Flame).
13. *Collected Works*, p.643 (Living Flame).
14. *Collected Works*, p.643 (Living Flame 1.7).
15. Brian Thorne, *Person Centred Counselling: Therapeutic and Spiritual Dimensions* (London: Whurr, 2000), p.76.
16. Donald Nicholl, *The Beatitude of Truth* (London: DLT, 1997), p.64.
17. Simone Weil, *Waiting on God* (Glasgow: Collins, 1951), pp.82–83.

18. For a fuller exploration of this theme see Ivan Mann, *A Double Thirst* (London: DLT, 2001).

Chapter 16: BETWEEN FIRE AND WATER

1. Iain Matthew, *The Impact of God* (London: Hodder and Stoughton, 1995), p.6.
2. ibid, p.9.
3. Elie Wiesel, *All Rivers Run to the Sea* (London: HarperCollins, 1997), p.178.

Copyright Acknowledgements

INDEX